# Winning Wealth Strategies

## *Secrets of Successful Investing in Any Market*

### Charles E. Mellon

**Sierra Newport Publishing, Inc.**
5015 West Sahara #125
Las Vegas, Nevada 89146

**Library of Congress No. 2001116837**

**ISBN # 0-9709524-0-6**

"This publication is designed to provide accurate and authoritative
information in regards to the subject matter covered. It is sold with the
understanding that the publisher is not engaged in rendering legal,
accounting, or other professional service. If legal or expert assistance is
required, the services of a competent professional person should be
sought."

*From the declaration principles jointly adopted by a committee of the
American Bar Association and a committee of the Publishers Association.*

Published in the United States by:

**Sierra Newport Publishing, Inc.**

5015 West Sahara #125
Las Vegas, Nevada 89146

# Table of Contents

Staging In

# Preface

This book is the result of over 25 years of my personal and professional investment experience. I started as a stockbroker in 1976, and quickly became one of the top producers in my firm (meaning, I helped my clients make a great deal of money). Over the years, I became a Branch Office Manager, and then Corporate Vice-President. (More important, I was making my clients a lot more money.) I became an expert in an entire range of investment vehicles, particularly those which generated *cash flow:* short-term gains on a daily and monthly basis, which added up to big yearly returns.

Many investors (including stockbrokers) avoided these short-term strategies because they considered things like options "too risky" and needing too much attention. However, I discovered that with some basic understanding, a certain amount of attention each day, and above all, clear ideas of my investment goals and the amount of risk I was willing to take, I could do very well with these strategies, both for my clients and myself.

I did so well, in fact, that in 1992 I left the stockbrokerage world to become a full-time investor. For the last nine years I have earned a very comfortable living doing exactly what you will learn in this book. I've made money in bull markets and bear markets; I've made money whether a stock's value went up or down. I've also learned when to get out of a particular investment (which can be even more important than when to get in). Many of the techniques I use are covered in these pages. Of course, I'm not right all the time, but I'm right more often than I'm wrong, and that's what makes the difference between a successful investor and one who's broke.

I'm not the only one who has profited from this information. In 1996 I started teaching what I practice to groups all around the world. Today I'm happy to say that investors in Europe, Australia, Canada, and the U.S. have taken these strategies and increased their returns on their investments, sometimes dramatically. And I want you to have the same opportunity.

You have taken the first step on your way to wealth by investing in this book. Much time, effort and research have gone into its pages. I hope it will be a truly useful guide, helping you to maximize your investment potential and overall portfolio returns. I've attempted to make the information and examples interesting and understandable so you will refer back to its pages again and again as you pursue your investment goals.

From the very start of my investment career, I loved being able to teach clients these winning wealth strategies. I still love giving people the kind of counsel that can unlock the doors to a new understanding of how to make their money work harder for them. This book is a summary of some of my best investment advice. By utilizing the methods in its pages and adhering to the basic strategies for portfolio management, you should dramatically increase your chances for future investment success. As you read this book, visualize the concepts being discussed, and ask yourself, "How can I use this to improve my own investment returns and overall financial position?"

May you enjoy the fruits of your efforts in the months and years ahead. Good luck investing!

*Winning Wealth Strategies*

# 1

# Creating Wealth

There have been hundreds, perhaps thousands, of books written on the subject of creating wealth. All have good ideas for readers to ponder as they make up their minds which step to take first. But the secret to wealth for the average person (if there is one) is fairly simple: *Spend less than you earn and invest the rest.*

If you work for a living, you essentially trade your productive daily hours for some kind of payment, usually in the form of hourly pay or a set salary. Once you know what you will make for a day's wages and after you deduct taxes, you have a certain sum left to live on. From that money, you have to provide food and shelter for yourself and your family; you have to pay for transportation, insurance, education, clothing, entertainment; you have to put aside something for a rainy day. Oh, yes—you also need to invest for your retirement.

And all of these costs must add up to *less* than you are earning. It's not that difficult a concept, yet many of us don't seem to understand the meaning of the phrase, "Spend less than you earn and invest the rest."

There is no simpler way for anyone —*anyone*—to become wealthy. By spending less than you earn and living modestly, it is quite possible for the average person to retire before the age of 65 with considerable assets. I'm sure you've heard stories about secretaries, farmers, UPS drivers, and others with modest incomes who achieved a fair degree of wealth simply by spending less than they earned and investing any extra capital in quality stocks over the long term. I personally know several individuals who have built million- and multimillion-dollar portfolios from modest monthly and annual investments over time. Whether it be in real estate, art, stocks or rare coins, **a continued investment program is essential to long-term financial independence.**

I'm not sure why there always seem to be a few people who think tomorrow will never come, but they certainly act as if that were true. How else can you explain the extravagant spending (and exorbitantly high debt) of many people in the U.S.? Huge homes (with huge mortgages) stuffed with designer furniture and state-of-the-art electronics; garages full of expensive foreign cars; men and women sporting expensive Swiss watches and the latest fashions; leisure activities like exotic vacations and country club memberships that cost thousands of dollars annually—conspicuous consumption seems to be the goal of every American. Nowhere else in the free world do you find this sort of excessive spending except in the United States, where we have the lowest savings rate as a percentage of income in the developed world.

It seems as though the U.S. motto is, "I want mine now, not later." Well, if that is indeed the case, there will be precious little left for the future. We cannot spend everything we earn now (and perhaps even more) and expect there to be adequate means for tomorrow. Large credit card and consumer debt usurp our ability to save and invest. If we continue as a society to spend far more than we earn, borrowing heavily to finance our whims and slightest desires, we will eventually see an economic downturn that will make the Great

Depression seem like a minor setback in comparison.

Control your spending! Save today! Invest well! Make a plan! This has been, and will continue to be, the recipe for wealth. You must temper your behavior and consumption. You must be determined and strong in your resolve to continue investing even when you don't want to. You must be careful to take calculated risks and not unnecessary risks. You must never invest the "rent money" or anything you cannot afford to lose. And you must be modestly self-assured that your efforts will be successful. None of these precepts have really changed since the beginning of time, but it seems that each generation must develop its own recognition of these principles.

When I speak to students and young investors, I remind them of something that our generation has perhaps forgotten: the *power of compounding*. Investing small amounts of money on a consistent basis over time can generate a huge amount of capital in 20 to 30 years. That may sound like a long time, but think about it: if you are 25 years old right now, you will be 45 or 50 when you enjoy the fruits of the investments you make today. If you are

45 years old and just starting an investment plan, you can still reap enormous benefits by the time you're 65.

Compounding makes use of three factors each investor must understand: *time*, *money*, and *rate of return*. Sometimes I use different examples when I show people compounding tables, but I've chosen two tables here that explain fairly well the dramatic benefits from consistent investment.

In the following tables, the amount of money invested is indicated by "$50/Month," "$100/Month," etc., and the amount of time by "1 Year," "5 Years," and so on. The rate of return—how much you wish to make each year on the money you invest—is either 15% in the first example, or 20% in the second. (You may believe that a 15% or 20% annual rate of return is high, but the techniques you will learn in this book will help you build a portfolio where those rates of return are relatively easy to achieve.)

# The Power of Compounding

## Table 1. 15% Annual Return

|            | 1 Year | 5 Years  | 10 Years | 20 Years  | 30 Years    |
|------------|--------|----------|----------|-----------|-------------|
| $50/Month  | $651   | $4,484   | $13,933  | $75,798   | $350,491    |
| $75/Month  | $977   | $6,726   | $20,899  | $113,697  | $525,737    |
| $100/Month | $1,302 | $8,968   | $27,866  | $151,596  | $700,982    |
| $150/Month | $1,953 | $13,452  | $41,799  | $227,393  | $1,051,473  |
| $200/Month | $2,604 | $17,936  | $55,731  | $303,191  | $1,401,964  |
| $250/Month | $3,255 | $22,420  | $69,664  | $378,989  | $1,752,455  |
| $300/Month | $3,906 | $26,904  | $83,597  | $454,787  | $2,102,946  |

# The Power of Compounding

## Table 2. 20% Annual Return

|            | 1 Year  | 5 Years  | 10 Years  | 20 Years  | 30 Years    |
|------------|---------|----------|-----------|-----------|-------------|
| $50/Month  | $669    | $5,173   | $19,118   | $158,074  | $1,168,040  |
| $75/Month  | $1,004  | $7,759   | $28,667   | $273,112  | $1,752,060  |
| $100/Month | $1,228  | $10,345  | $38,236   | $316,148  | $2,336,080  |
| $150/Month | $2,007  | $15,518  | $57,355   | $474,222  | $3,504,120  |
| $200/Month | $2,677  | $20,691  | $76,473   | $632,296  | $4,672,160  |
| $250/Month | $3,346  | $25,864  | $95,591   | $790,370  | $5,840,200  |
| $300/Month | $4,015  | $31,036  | $114,709  | $948,444  | $7,008,241  |

As you can see from the tables, the more time you have, the less money you need to invest in order to reach a certain amount. The less time you have, the more money you will need to achieve that same financial goal. And if you can increase your rate of return, you can reach your financial goals much faster with less money.

But to utilize the power of compounding, you still need *some* money to invest—and unless you win the lottery, or inherit capital, or stumble across a wad of cash somebody dropped in your path, you have to *spend less than you earn and invest the rest*. And the sooner you do so, the more quickly you can start investing your way to wealth.

# Section I

# The Foundations of
# Successful Investing

The chapters in this section are designed to give you a basic understanding of the securities markets in the United States. These fundamentals will help you build a foundation for the more advanced strategies and techniques covered later.

As an investor, there are two issues you must address before you put money into anything. First, look at your *tolerance for risk*. Every investment carries with it some level of risk. Your comfort with the emotional ups and downs of investing will have a large impact on the investments you choose and the returns you receive.

Second, look at *the way you choose to build your investment portfolio*—what you buy and sell, how much, and when. Issues like diversification, asset allocation, appropriate investments given your individual goals, all come into play. It is important to understand what goes into your portfolio before we speak about ways to make more money with what you have.

I am primarily a short-term, momentum investor focusing on stocks and options, and most of the strategies in this book use those kinds of investments. However, there are other financial instruments that are found in the average investor's portfolio—mutual funds and U.S. Treasuries. I want to provide some explanation of how these financial instruments work, and how you can evaluate them intelligently. Therefore, in this section you'll find chapters addressing these financial instruments.

My goal in this section—indeed, with the entire book—is for you to feel in control of your financial life. I believe it is up to you to learn how to evaluate investments intelligently, gathering all the information you can to maximize your returns. Happily, with a relatively small amount of study, research, and understanding, you can master the winning wealth strategies in this book.

# 2

# What's Your
# Risk Tolerance?

No one really likes to take a lot of risk with their money. Sure, we're willing to take high returns; we just don't want to take any undue risk to achieve them! So how do we determine what the proper risk level is for us, and what investments may be appropriate given that risk level?

It's easier than you might imagine to determine what our particular risk level *should* be; it's a lot more difficult to determine what our risk level actually *is*. I could dedicate this entire book to risk tolerance, but it wouldn't change anyone's mind about what's appropriate for him or her. Your father or grandfather might think investing in anything other than CDs and Treasury bonds is very risky. Conversely, your 25-year-old co-worker may have her entire IRA invested in Internet stocks. What's extremely risky for your next-door neighbor might seem like a walk in the park to you.

We all have our own ideas as to what risk is, and nothing that anyone else says is going to change our minds. Basically, that's because we are investing *our* money, not someone else's, and no one is coming to our rescue should we lose money in the process of listening to someone else's advice. So, let's take a look at risk as a manageable factor. We start by identifying our own risk tolerance level so we can use it to our advantage.

# Determining Your Risk Tolerance

There's a very familiar phrase that many people use when they talk about risk: they judge risk tolerance by how well they sleep at night. I believe this is a good benchmark, since we can all relate to the nights where we tossed and turned, second-guessing an investment decision, asking, "How in the heck could I have been so stupid as to do that?" So, in looking at your own risk tolerance for a particular investment (or category of investments), always ask yourself, "How will I sleep if I put my money into this? Can I handle the risk?" And don't just say, "Sure—no problem!" Take a few moments to really evaluate how you will manage the *emotions* of this investment. Remember, most people lose money because they let their emotions dictate their investment decisions. They see a stock going down and they sell in a panic, even though they have analyzed the company and know it has strong financials and solid underlying value. Or they hang onto a stock because they "just know" it will go back up again, even though the company just declared its earnings are going south and the CEO has just resigned. Managing your emotions—including your tolerance for risk—is a very important investment skill.

So, how do you determine your own risk tolerance? Let me tell you a story that will help. Suppose you had worked hard for 20 years and that you're now 40 years old. You have a family to support, a mortgage payment, a car payment, MasterCard and Visa payments, and all the other expenses related to children nearing college age. Suppose, further, that you and your spouse have been able to save an extra $10,000 in cash. Those funds are not allocated to pending educational needs, medical or dental expenses, insurance, vacations, or other household related expenses. Naturally you don't want to lose that $10,000, but if you did, it wouldn't dramatically change your lifestyle or keep you from enjoying the sunset.

One day you get a call from Tom, your stockbroker, who recommends a particular stock, XYZ, as a short-term investment. Without discussing it with your spouse, you ask Tom to use the entire $10,000 to buy 1,000 shares of the stock at $10 a share. Later that day, he calls to confirm the purchase. "You bought the stock at $10 on the ask side of the market," he says. "It's still in that area, but the last trade was $9.75." *Oops,* you think, *It's gone down a little already. Oh well, I can handle it.* (If you don't understand the broker's language, don't worry—we'll cover that in Chapter 11, "Stock Terms.")

That night at the dinner table, after the children have left to do their homework, you casually say to your spouse, "By the way, honey, I bought some shares in XYZ Company. Our stockbroker thinks it's got good upside potential in the near term."

"How much did you spend?" your spouse asks.

"I bought 1,000 shares at $10 each. It's a really good investment," you reply reassuringly.

Your spouse is uncharacteristically silent at this point, continuing to push the food around on his or her dinner plate. As you get up to leave the table at the end of the meal, your spouse says, "I really wish you had let me be part of your decision to invest all of our savings. I just hope everything turns out all right." Neither of you mentions the investment for the rest of the evening.

*(How are you doing? Any problems sleeping so far?)*

At the office the next day you're preoccupied with work, but around three o'clock you remember the stock you bought the day before. "I wonder how the market is doing?" you say as you turn on the radio and tune to the local business station. Just then, you hear a report that the Federal Reserve Board was considering an increase in the discount rate. Traders on Wall Street are worried that interest rates might go up again. As a result, they have begun "lightening up" their portfolios. (In Wall Street jargon that means they are selling probably 25% of what they own in stocks.) This sell off is causing a large drop in the Dow Jones Industrial Average (DJIA). Not being sure what all this means, you decide to call your broker just to get an idea where your stock is trading in relation to the overall market.

"Well," Tom says, "An increase in the discount rate means higher interest costs for businesses and individuals, because banks will probably raise their prime lending rates. Bond prices would decline to increase yields to investors. Unfortunately, stock prices are following suit."

"I understand," you reply. "But tell me: what's the price of that stock I bought yesterday?"

"Even though the market's down about 60 points today, your stock is holding up very well, all things considered," Tom reassures you. "It's currently trading at about $8.50 per share, but it seems to be stabilizing at that level. Don't worry."

That night when we get home from work, your spouse casually asks, "Hey, I heard the market dropped 60 points today. How's our stock doing?"

"I never knew you were interested in the market," you mumble. "We've been married 18 years and we've never discussed it before." You change the subject quickly, and your spouse lets it drop. You both go to bed without any further discussion on investments.

*(How do you feel now? Are you still confident about your decision?)*

As luck would have it, the very next day the Chairman of the Federal Reserve Board announces an increase in the discount rate of 1/2%. *Not too bad,* you think. *I wonder how it is affecting the market?* Unable to contain yourself, you pick up the phone and call Tom.

"The market didn't react very favorably to the rate increase," he says. "It came rather unexpectedly, and conventional analysis had indicated a 1/4-point increase as the probable maximum. Wall Street wasn't prepared for a 1/2-point rate increase, and that caused a lot more selling than usual. I'm afraid we're in for some more bloodletting over the near term, but after that the market should probably stabilize."

"What about XYZ?" you ask.

"It's been subjected to additional selling, too. Right now it's off about 3/4 of a point." (*Off* means down in the investment business. They use that word because it sounds better than the word *down*.)

"3/4 of a point doesn't sound so bad," you say. "What would I get if I were to sell at this level?"

"Let's see—the last trade on the stock was $7.75, down 3/4 of a point from yesterday, but if you were to sell the stock, you'd only get the bid price, which is $7.25," Tom reports.

"Thanks for the information," you reply, too stunned to say anything more intelligent, and too confused to ask further questions about the market. *I've only had this stock for a few days and already I've lost nearly $3,000,* you think nervously.

Unable to concentrate fully on your business, you decide to go home early to spend some quality time with your family. As soon as you walk in the front door you realize with a sinking feeling that your spouse has returned home from work early as well.

"Are you okay?" your spouse asks. "This is the first time in nearly ten years you've come home this early. Anything bothering you?"

"I finished a project in less time than I expected, that's all," you say. "I wanted to spend some time with my family." Everything seems to be going well until the six o'clock news comes on television. The whole family watches as the TV commentator reports, "The Dow Jones Industrial Average closed down 165 points today in very heavy trading." Immediately, the head of every family member swivels toward you, looking for your reaction to this news. They know you have recently purchased stock for the benefit of the entire family so that Junior can go to that special college, you can put in the swimming pool like your neighbors, and maybe you and your spouse can take that second honeymoon.

Mustering all your thespian abilities, you reassure your family, "I spoke to our broker today and he said our investment was off just a little." (You, too, use the word *off*, realizing your family probably has no idea that it really means *down*.) The explanation seems to go over very well and the rest of the night passes pleasantly. You feel a little guilty about misleading your family about the stock's value, *but it'll probably come right back up tomorrow,* you think, as you head to bed.

*(How are you feeling at this point? Can you still sleep all right? Do you feel confident that you made the right decision even though your timing might not have been perfect? Can you live with a "paper loss" of 30% of your money? )*

"Nothing goes down forever," you say to yourself while driving to work. "I'm going to call Tom as soon as I get to the office and get an early morning update." After stopping at a customer's place of business on the way to work, you arrive near your usual time and trot into the office with a determined and confident air. As soon as your secretary sees you, however, she flags you down. "Urgent," you hear, then something about "call your broker immediately." You go directly into your office without stopping for your usual cup of coffee, and dial the telephone before you sit down. You drop your car keys on the desk loudly, nearly knocking over the chair in your attempt to jump into your seat. Then Tom comes on the line.

"The market was waiting for some news about XYZ," he tells you. "That news was released this morning before the market opened, and unfortunately, it wasn't nearly as good as we'd hoped: the company's sales for the last quarter have been much lower than expected."

You swallow hard. "What do you recommend, Tom?" you ask.

"I'd suggest that you sell the stock when the market opens for trading. Most analysts are now putting a near-term 'sell' recommendation on this stock. That's sure to affect XYZ's future upside potential in a negative way."

"What's the current price?" you ask.

"Well, because of the news, XYZ's stock has been temporarily suspended from trading. When it opens back up I'll have a price for you . . . . Wait a minute, it just opened for trading." After a few seconds, he reports, "XYZ is now bid at $5 per share and volume appears to be very heavy. That's not a good sign," he adds. "It may go even lower."

Not being able to make yourself take a $5,000 loss this early in the morning, you instruct your broker to wait until you call him with further instructions. You have a sinking feeling in the pit of your stomach; you close the door to your office and tell your secretary not to disturb you unless the boss calls.

*(Can you hold up in the face of adversity? Will you "tough it out" no matter what? Think you'll be able to sleep tonight?)*

That evening one of your neighbors drops by unexpectedly after dinner. You are cordial (he's been your neighbor for more than ten years) and casually invite him into the house for a chat. You start talking about current events, and the subject of the stock market comes up. Your neighbor mentions that he heard about a publicly-traded company that competes with ABC, the company he works for. This competitor recently came out with an earnings report that was disastrous. "We're going to put them out of business," he crows. Suddenly, you realize he's talking about XYZ. You rapidly put two and two together (yes, you do get four) and decide to exploit this conversation to find out more about the company.

"It's poorly run—bad management," your neighbor says. "They make a good product but can't seem to get it to market on time. Glad I don't own any of *their* stock," he chortles. "I'd do myself in."

At this point you get up off the couch and say, "Gee, Bob, it sure was nice of you to stop over. Wish you could stay longer, but I know how busy you are. Come again another time, won't you? Goodnight!" Your neighbor is a bit surprised but he leaves.

Your spouse thinks that was rather abrupt of you, but nothing further is said about it until bedtime. "Is there something wrong?" your spouse wonders aloud. "You seem on edge lately."

"Just tired," you respond, "I'm going to bed."

*(How do you feel now? Can you handle the pressure? Still able to sleep at night? Hang in there—we're not done yet.)*

The next morning you call your broker from the office right after the market opens and inquire about your position. "Hey, buddy," Tom says, "I told you to sell yesterday when the stock was at $5.

As of now, the bid is at $3.85." You sit back in shock. You have a "paper loss" (not a real loss unless you sell) of nearly 70% of your investment, excluding commission charges.

"What would you like to do?" Tom inquires.

"Nothing. I'll call you," you reply, hanging up on him. Wishing you had talked this investment over with your spouse first (at least then you would have someone to share the blame), you spend the day trying to figure out how to break the news to your family. After all, it certainly wasn't your fault; the market is to blame for this loss. And who can predict the stock market?

The family is quiet at the dinner table that evening. It's as if they can sense you're about to say something that might change their lives. But you can't muster the courage to say anything. You go to bed hoping that tomorrow might bring better news.

*(Can you live with it? You* are *tough!)*

The next morning, after a loss of 250 points over the previous four trading days, the market rebounds, with the DJIA opening up 50 points.

Hearing this on the radio, you immediately dial your broker and ask about your stock.

"It's still the same as yesterday," he says.

"But how can that be?" you implore. "The market is up 50 points; surely my stock will be up today. Are you sure you're getting accurate quotes on my stock? You have to be mistaken."

"The Dow stocks are going higher because of the recent marketwide sell-off," your broker explains. "It's a rebound effect and probably won't last. The market has broken its trend line and it will probably continue to decline over the near term. You should get out now. The bid on XYZ is $3, and that's the best you're going to do in this market."

Not feeling too well now, you thank him for his time and mention that you will probably take his advice, but first you must discuss it with the family. "I thought you were going to do that a couple of days ago," the broker interjects. Feeling helpless and alone, you thank the broker again and hang up. Tonight, you decide, you will definitely tell your family the truth.

At the dinner table, you can't eat. You have to tell the others about the predicament you've gotten everyone into. There will be no swimming pool, no special college for Junior, and no second honeymoon. Everything is going to evaporate into thin air because of your mistakes in judgment, and your obstinate holding on to a stock that was sure to go down the drain.

"I have an announcement to make," you say, as the family looks up in wonder. At that moment, the doorbell rings. Your spouse goes to answer it before you can finish your sentence (and your confession). At the door is your neighbor, Bob, smiling brightly. He walks straight into your dining room and exclaims, "You are now looking at the president of a new division of ABC. Remember that company we were talking about the other night, XYZ—the one that had such poor management and all? Well, my company just agreed to buy it. You'll be hearing the news on TV any minute now. The exchange stopped trading in the shares late this afternoon pending the announcement, but my company is buying XYZ for $18 per share."

You look at your neighbor in complete shock. "It's worth $18 a share?" you ask.

"Yep," he answers. "If you owned the stock you could have made a fortune. It was trading as low as $3 today."

"I do own it; or we do—our family, I mean," you reply with a huge smile. "That's the announcement I was just about to make to the family before you came in. We nearly doubled our money in just two weeks!" Your family cheers as you continue, "I was just going to tell everyone that we're going to put in a swimming pool like you have next door." And you sit back, feeling relieved and overwhelmed with your sudden good fortune.

The next day you call your broker and sell the stock at $17.50 per share, a $7,500 profit in two weeks' time. But in truth, you're just glad that you were able to get out of a terrible situation, from which you were fortunately rescued by fate.

\* \* \* \* \* \* \* \* \*

Based on your response to the story, what's your risk tolerance? Would you have sold after the first decline? the second? the third? When it reached $3 (a 70% loss on your investment)? Would you have been able to sleep each night?

If you believe you could weather that large drop in price without panic and without loss of sleep, you have a very high level of risk tolerance. You should have no problem making intelligent, unemotional decisions regarding your investments. However, if you had immediate problems with the poor news on the company and the subsequent drop in stock price to $5, you have a very low risk tolerance, and should be careful about the *types* of investments you choose (we'll discuss which types in Sections II, III, and IV) and the *amount of money* you invest in stocks.

If you fall in the middle ground—you were moderately concerned about your situation until the end of the above example—you have a better than average risk tolerance. You should do very well investing in the stock market for the long and short term, using the guidelines you'll find in the rest of this book.

# 3

# Profitable
# Portfolio
# Management

Everyone seeks to make the most from his or her investment dollars. Not all of us do, though, because we disregard basic investment philosophy whenever we get caught up in the fervor of stock market investing. Most of us *know what to do* to generate decent investment returns; we just don't always *do what we know*. We violate basic tenets of investing and disregard some of the cardinal rules of successful investment philosophy.

In this book you will learn the basic strategies of investing for profit. These strategies include techniques for both short-term *and* long-term investing, to assure that the bulk of your portfolio remains intact during market setbacks (which will inevitably occur from time to time).

Let's begin by describing the two basic types of investing. These categories apply whether you're putting your money into mutual funds, individual stocks, options or other derivatives, U.S. Treasuries—indeed, almost every kind of investment. And, as we'll discuss at the end of the chapter, both investment types have their places in your overall financial portfolio.

# Buy and Hold

The first type of investment strategy is called *buy and hold,* which means exactly that: you buy stock and hold onto it. Obviously, buy and hold is a *long-term* strategy within your overall goal of managing your portfolio for maximum returns.

When you look for a buy and hold stock, choose companies using the following criteria:

> ➤ A long history of *strong earnings* (at least three to five years' worth)

> ➤ A stock that pays *dividends* (which you can then invest, either in that stock or in other stocks)

> ➤ A company that *dominates its product or industry category*

Buy and hold stocks are usually referred to as *blue chip* stocks. You'll learn more about choosing buy and hold stocks in Section II of this book, "Stocks: The Basics."

# Momentum Investing

The second category of investment strategies deals with *short-term* investing—as short as one to two days, or as long as three months or more. I will refer to these short-term strategies as *momentum investing,* because they take advantage of the momentum (either up or down) of the stock market. Momentum investing is an excellent way to create ongoing cash flow in your portfolio, which you then can reinvest, thereby creating greater returns.

Many momentum stocks can be high quality and still be considered second or third tier in the market as a whole. Why? Companies with excellent products and bright futures are still considered lower-tier because they are small in terms of *market capitalization* (market value of all outstanding stock). Nearly all companies start in this category before their sales reach a billion dollars or more. I consider a company to be a potential "high-flyer" when it possesses some current economic or technological advantage over another company, industry or sector of the market.

Please note, however: to take advantage of momentum investing, you must be aware of the *daily* movements of the marketplace. You cannot bury your head in the sand and wait for your stocks to rise (as you can with many buy and hold investments). Momentum investing strategies carry greater risks, but they also can produce much greater returns. You'll learn several momentum investing strategies in Sections III and IV.

# Determining Your Portfolio Mix

Before using any strategy or technique, you must first determine your *portfolio mix:* how much of your portfolio will be allocated to longer-term buy and hold investments and how much to short-term momentum investing. Most people usually figure this out by assessing how much risk they are willing to take and how much "action" they require to satisfy their need for excitement. However, if you use emotion to determine your portfolio mix, you'll probably get great emotional returns but not much else. Deciding your investments based on emotion isn't investing, it's gambling, and you'd be very foolish to do so.

Most professional portfolio managers use two criteria to determine the best stock portfolio mix for a client. I recommend you use the same criteria when creating your own portfolio.

## 1. Investor Age

Most of us have to do some kind of work to accumulate money (capital) with which to invest, and we each have a certain number of years to earn a productive income. As we get older, however, we have less and less time in which to earn income that can be used for investment capital. If we make mistakes in our investment portfolio—we choose a "hot" stock in a company which then goes bankrupt, for example—we will have less time to replace the money we lost. This means that the older you get, the more conservative your investments should be.

## 2. Investment Capital

The second criterion involves the amount of money you have available to invest. You can start investing with any amount of capital, from $500 on up. Of course, the more money you have to invest, the more risk you can take within your portfolio, simply because you can replenish any short-term losses from your capital.

Although it is not a hard and fast rule, I recommend the following formula of stock investment allocation for most people.

### Table 1: Investment Allocation by Age

| Below age 25 | **10%** Buy & Hold | **90%** Momentum |
|---|---|---|
| Ages 25 to 35 | **25%** Buy & Hold | **75%** Momentum |
| Ages 35 to 50 | **50%** Buy & Hold | **50%** Momentum |
| Ages 50 to 65 | **75%** Buy & Hold | **25%** Momentum |
| Ages 65+ | **90%** Buy & Hold | **10%** Momentum |

Please note: these guidelines refer to the part of your portfolio that is dedicated to stocks.

Say you are 30 years old and want to start investing. Based on the table, your stock portfolio would be allocated 25% to buy and hold, and 75%

to momentum. If you are 55 years old, you'd allocate 75% to buy and hold and 25% to momentum—a more conservative mix. (A 55-year-old has less time than the 30-year-old to recoup his or her losses from unsuccessful investments.)

There are three caveats to the Investment Allocation by Age table. First, you'll notice that the age groups overlap by a year. If you're at the top or bottom of one of the age groups (25, 35, 50, 65), you should use the more conservative formula if you are a conservative investor by nature or feel you might be subject to early retirement or layoff in the ensuing years.

Second, the investment allocations for ages 55 and older assume that you are currently working and will not be subject to income interruption or early retirement. If you are not working, or are planning an early retirement, you should use the more conservative investment allocation ratios.

Third, if you have specific goals, like funding your retirement, your portfolio mix will also depend on how much money you have available to invest. If you're 50 years old and have only $10,000 to invest, putting it all into long-term buy and hold stocks probably won't provide the capital growth you need to create a sufficient retirement fund by the time you're 65 or even 70. Therefore, you would need to increase the percentage allocated to momentum strategies, and decrease the percentage for buy and hold investments. In exchange for the greater risk you will have the possibility of greater returns, which can turn your $10,000 into a sufficient nest egg faster.

(Although there are no set recommended standards for age versus investment capital, the Power of Compounding tables in Chapter 1 will show how much money can be generated over time given a particular annual rate of return from investments. These tables can help you determine allocation percentages as well.)

Using the Investment Allocation by Age table on page 34, take a moment to find your optimum portfolio mix and write it down for future reference. In later portions of this book you can begin building a portfolio for yourself by using this percentage ratio. Although the tables contained in this book are only suggested guidelines, using them can help prevent unnecessary hardship during the natural ups and downs of the market.

# 4

# Diversification Essentials

Whether for purposes of income or growth, maximum "cash flow" is an oft-stated goal of investors. Naturally, people want to make as much money as possible from their investment dollars. But if this objective is foremost in their minds, it can cause them to completely disregard Mom's old warning, "Don't put all your eggs in one basket." And investors ignore the key principle of *diversification* at their peril.

Here's a common example. You get a tip from your neighbor that "MNOP's" stock is sure to go through the roof. In your excitement to get in on the stock before its expected price soar, the next day you use $50,000 of the money in your IRA to buy MNOP stock. You know it isn't prudent for you to invest the whole $50,000 in one stock, but you hope to make a real killing and then go back to more conservative practices. "Just this once and never again," you say to yourself. "I want to make a big hit and then I'll be more cautious." Well, it seems like every time you do this, it proves to be the wrong time or the wrong investment. That's why the importance of diversification as part of portfolio management cannot be overstated.

Although we never like to think that any of our investment decisions will be bad—our stocks will perform poorly, or our bonds will be downgraded in rating—history says otherwise. Diversification helps protect us from having the consequences of one bad investment destroy our entire portfolio.

# What's Your Diversification Mix?

In the process of diversifying your portfolio, you may wish to use the following tables as a guide. They give percentages for the mix of equity (stocks) and debt (bonds) securities in diversified portfolios, based on your age and the kind of growth you wish to pursue—aggressive or conservative. (Remember our discussion from Chapter 2: aggressive growth usually brings with it greater risk, while conservative growth means less risk but lower returns on average.) Diversifying your portfolio based on these tables should help you maintain your assets even during difficult times in the market.

## AGGRESSIVE

| Age 25 to 35 | 100% Equity | 0% Bonds |
|---|---|---|
| Age 35 to 50 | 75% Equity | 25% Bonds |
| Age 50 to 55 | 65% Equity | 35% Bonds |
| Age 55 to 65 | 50% Equity | 50% Bonds |
| Age 65+ | 35% Equity | 65% Bonds |

### vs.

## CONSERVATIVE

| Age 25 to 35 | 90% Equity | 10% Bonds |
|---|---|---|
| Age 35 to 50 | 75% Equity | 25% Bonds |
| Age 50 to 55 | 50% Equity | 50% Bonds |
| Age 55 to 65 | 35% Equity | 65% Bonds |
| Age 65+ | 15% Equity | 85% Bonds |

Based on these tables, if you were a 36-year-old investor and you wanted aggressive growth, you would put 90% of your portfolio in equities (stocks) and 10% in bonds. If you wanted a more conservative mix, you would put 75% in stocks, and 25% in bonds.

Two things to note about these tables. First, they indicate diversification ratios of stocks and bonds only; they do not address proper diversification *within* each part of the portfolio. You must also make sure that your stock and bond holdings are well diversified.

**I always suggest that investors put no more than 20% of their holdings in any one security.** That applies to portfolios of average size. The larger the portfolio, however, the *greater* the need for additional diversification. A $100,000 portfolio may be adequately diversified with five or six separate issues, but a $1,000,000 portfolio would require even further diversification—15 to 20 or more different issues. When in doubt, know that it is far better to over-diversify than to do otherwise.

Second, the percentage totals in the preceding tables represent the proper allocation for only that portion of your portfolio that is invested at any given time. **I recommend that you always keep part of your portfolio in cash.** This will help insulate you against a catastrophic market downturn, as well as making funds available for future investment opportunities.

As I said earlier, we will all make investment mistakes. Certainly, the market and the economy are guaranteed to fluctuate, perhaps wildly, during the course of your investing years. Proper diversification can make the difference between a prosperous portfolio and financial ruin. It will also help you sleep a little more soundly at night, because you will know that your assets are protected from the market, from the economy—and from yourself.

# 5

# Rules for
# Investment Success

Let's discuss ways for staying out of trouble with investments by laying some ground rules for the average investor. One of the questions I hear most often is, "When do I sell to take my profit?" My standard tongue-in-cheek answer is, "How much money do you want to make?" That's because there is no set answer for how much money you can or should be making with any particular trade. Every investor's goal is for profitable trades to run up as much as possible, and unprofitable trades to be nipped in the bud quickly.

Through the years I've developed some guidelines for successful investing. These are not proprietary to me, but based on common sense and common knowledge. By following these guidelines, you stand a good chance of maximizing your profit on the majority of your trades.

## 1. Do Your Homework

First and foremost, you must do your homework before you purchase the stock. Have you done the necessary research on this stock from both a fundamental and technical perspective? Do you know enough about the company to decide whether on not you should own it? Many people rely on hearsay or the uninformed opinions of someone else to determine whether or not to buy, but that is pure gambling. As an investor, you must be able to determine what the prospects for a company are before deciding to buy. To determine that, you must know quite a bit about the company.

A lot of what you need to know you can find on the Internet. One of the most popular sites for company information is Yahoo! Finance. You can also see dedicated financial sites like Quicken, your brokerage's Web site, or sites run by the company you want to research. (We'll cover what you need to know at a minimum in Chapter 8.)

## 2. Know Your Defense Strategy

After determining when to buy, you must prepare a defense strategy. How and when are you going to get out should the investment not work out

*web site*

*stop loss*

the way you've planned? (I can tell you from experience, investments don't work out about 30 to 40% of the time.) You need to establish a *loss limit*—the point at which you will sell the investment no matter what. I usually use **10% of the price of the stock:** I will sell immediately if the price of the stock drops 10% below the price where I purchased it.

To make sure you limit your losses, at the same time you confirm the initial purchase of the stock you should place a *sell-stop order* at 10% below the current market value, using an "open" or GTC (*Good 'Til Cancel*) order. An open or GTC order will stay on the books until you, as the seller, cancel it. A GTC order means that if the stock price ever drops below the price you have set, your broker will sell the stock immediately, without having to confirm the order with you. By using an open sell-stop order, you limit your losses on any particular stock to approximately 10%. This technique of limiting the downside (or potential loss) of your investments is at least as important as maximizing your upside when it comes to the value of your portfolio. (You'll learn more about sell-stops in Chapter 11, "Stock Terms.")

## 3. Know Your Time Frame & Stick to It

For every investment, you must know how long you plan to hold onto this stock. Is this a buy and hold stock in a solid company whose value you expect to increase significantly over the long run? Or is this a momentum stock, where your goal is to make money on an upcoming piece of news and then get out? Whatever your intention is, you must hold to it. If you buy ABC stock thinking that when earnings are announced next week the stock should move up and then you can sell for a profit, *sell the stock after the earnings are announced, no matter what.* If the earnings aren't as good as expected or the stock doesn't move up, then your original premise was wrong, and everything after that premise is wrong, too. Sell the stock no matter what—holding on to it in hopes of making a profit "some day" has made many a rich person a lot poorer. Admit your miscalculation and move on to other, more profitable opportunities.

If your original premise is correct and the stock moves up, deciding when to take profits is critical. This is when we use the sell-stop order (as we'll discuss in Chapter 11) to protect profits while letting the stock run up as much as possible.

## Some Additional Notes for Options Trades

I want to mention options here, even though I will be discussing options trading in great detail in Section III. In the case of options investing, it is even *more* critical to stand by your original premise to protect yourself from loss. Options move in a magnified nature percentage-wise, so any up or down movement in a stock's price can cause big swings in the value of the option on that stock (which we love—it's called leverage). So, in the event you purchase an option with the hope that a particular news item would move the underlying stock up, if that stock doesn't move higher, then the options will lose value quickly.

**I set my maximum loss on option purchases at 50% of the price I paid for the option.** If I bought ten contracts of options on ABCD for $3, for example, if the price of the option dropped to $1 1/2, I would sell it immediately. I would take a 50% loss, but I would avoid losing the entire investment should the value of the option drop to zero (which can happen).

Conversely, if the option *increases* in price, I would look to protect my profits by selling the original dollar amount of my investment plus a reasonable profit, and let the remaining number of options "ride." Here's what I mean. Say I bought ten option contracts at $3, and the options are now selling for $5. I would probably sell eight of the contracts (thereby recouping my original investment plus a reasonable profit) and keep the other two. This way, if the options continue to go up, I can profit on the two contracts remaining. I would most likely sell the two contracts when the option price tripled, or when the time remaining before expiration date was one week or less. On the other hand, if something negative happened to the option price in the future, I have no real investment risk, only an opportunity loss, since I have already taken my profits on this trade.

If you find the discussion above somewhat confusing, don't worry. You will learn about options trading in Section III. In the meantime, just remember: hold to your original premise and time frame when executing a momentum trade, and you'll keep yourself out of a whole lot of trouble.

# 6

# Mutual Funds

Many people (if not most) feel that mutual fund investing is the way to play the stock market with limited risk. With the professional management and diversification that are hallmarks of most mutual funds, investors relax and feel comfortable, because they believe their mutual funds will achieve a return equal to or better than any other type of investment.

This is not necessarily true. Yes, mutual funds are an excellent vehicle for the small investor who wishes to put some money into stocks for long-term growth. Because of their nature and size, most mutual funds do diversify an investment portfolio. Fund investors do not always recognize the *costs* of professional management and fund diversification, though. And these costs usually manifest in lower returns than individuals could achieve by investing in the stock market on their own.

Each mutual fund has administrative expenses, commission costs and management fees, etc., and these costs vary greatly from fund to fund. Performance will also vary from fund to fund, and from fund family to fund family. Each fund's prospectus spells out in detail the fees and expected expenses in any given period. Also, each fund is required to make earnings, net asset, and performance reports available to existing investors annually (with quarterly updates), and to provide potential investors with similar information. If you wish to put part of your investment capital into a mutual fund, you should read these reports and the prospectus carefully before deciding to invest.

I believe there are a couple of problems with mutual fund investing. Have you seen the disclaimer in mutual fund ads: "Past performance is no indication of future earnings"? By law, mutual fund advertisers must include that phrase because it's true: a mutual fund's overall return last year is no indication of how profitable it will be in the future. Also, many good mutual funds fall victim to their own success. For example, if ABC fund has great returns for a while, more people then put their money in. But as ABC grows in size, it can't be as flexible in taking advantage of moves in the stock market, and therefore its performance may decline—sometimes dramatically.

**Mutual funds can rarely outperform disciplined individuals who adhere to proven methods and are willing to do their own investigation and research.** A mutual fund with an annual return to investors of 20% is quite good—but I believe (and you'll see demonstrated in this book) that informed individual investors who make their own decisions can do much *better* than an annual return of 20%.

Mutual funds do have a place in your overall investment portfolio, however. An Individual Retirement Account (IRA), for example, is a good place for investing in mutual funds. With an annual commitment of only $2,000, it would be hard to get the same diversification with any other investment vehicle. Mutual funds, therefore, probably make sense in many IRAs.

When you choose a mutual fund, you must scrutinize it carefully, to make sure that the fund's performance and investment objectives are commensurate with your own. Many funds put money into risky investments in very volatile stocks, in an effort to improve overall fund performance. You must be very aware of how a fund manager regards these types of investments, and what actions are taken to protect investors (from a fund manager's viewpoint) should the market take a quick reversal.

**When in doubt, talk to the fund's representative.** Each fund has an investor relations department (and usually a regional representative) that is prepared to answer questions from individual investors regarding the fund's performance and investment objectives. A phone call to investor relations may very well soothe whatever reservations or concerns you may have about a particular fund—or may keep you out of an unsound fund to begin with.

There are rating services available, too, which you can rely on to help make investment decisions. *Morningstar* is perhaps the most comprehensive mutual fund rating service. It can give you both the details and an assessment of a fund's performance versus its investment risk, the overall fund volatility, and many other important factors that will help you choose wisely. *Morningstar* reports are available from your stockbroker, at your local library, and online at "Morningstarreports.com." Proper use of this type of information can and will save you from making uninformed decisions that can hurt long-term investment performance.

# Choosing a Mutual Fund

I recommend using the following criteria when choosing a mutual fund. They give a good picture of the financial health of a fund, and allow for comparison of one fund to another. All this information can be found in *Morningstar*, or in a fund's prospectus.

## 1. Total Return

The first thing I look for is *total return*. How much money would I have made if I had bought this fund on January first? I want to know the fund's overall performance in percentage terms, too, so I can compare it to other funds. Then I like to see the one-, three-, five- and ten-year total returns to get an idea of how consistent the fund manager's performance and judgment have been. (Total returns through the years are excellent tools for comparing one fund to another.)

**Note:** Beware the fund that has had a huge gain in the last twelve months yet poor returns in the last three to five years. Anyone can get lucky in the market in the short term, but that doesn't necessarily mean you'd want to invest with them—they might not be so lucky in the future.

## 2. Investment Objective

The second thing I look for is the investment objective of the fund. Does it focus on dividend-paying stocks, holding them for long-term gains? Or is it more of a short-term trading fund, comprised of high-risk technology sector and biotech stocks? I want the fund to have the same objectives I do in my own stock purchases.

## 3. Beta

Beta is the relative volatility of the fund when compared to the market as a whole. A beta of 1.0 means that the fund's volatility is equal to the overall market. A beta of, say, 0.75, indicates the fund is 25% less volatile than the overall market. Conversely, a beta of more than 1.0 means the fund is more volatile than the market as a whole.

When looking at beta, you need to know your own investment objective for this fund. If you're a conservative investor who's ten years from retirement, you may want a stable, non-volatile investment, so you'd look for a fund whose beta is less than 1.0—perhaps 0.6 or 0.7. These kinds of funds are called *balanced funds*, with significant holdings in bonds, or perhaps they would be utilities funds or income funds.

Now, say you want to set up an education account for your new child or grandchild. The child won't need the money for 15 to 18 years, but you'd like to get the most "bang" for your investment buck. So you might look for an aggressive growth fund, for example, with a beta of 1.0 or more. A fund with a beta over 1.0 is going to move *more* than the market, so you can benefit with greater returns if the market rises. At the same time, you know your investment goal is far enough away to recoup any losses if the market drops.

One caveat, however: invest in funds with betas over 1.0 only if you're putting money in over time—a certain amount each year, for example. That way, you benefit from the principle of *dollar cost averaging* (see Glossary) and lower your potential for loss. If you're putting a lump sum in a mutual fund, I don't recommend investing in one with a beta of over 1.0.

## 4. Major Holdings

I always want to know about the fund's major portfolio holdings. Which stocks does this fund choose to put (my) money in? Major portfolio holdings for each mutual fund are listed in *Morningstar*, and in the prospectus the fund is required to give investors before they buy. I like to look for major holdings in stocks and companies I'm familiar with, because they give me confidence in the management of the fund. (If the fund management likes many of the same stocks that I do, obviously they're doing a great job!)

After I look at total return, investment objective, beta, and major holdings, I then evaluate using the following criteria, which can be given different weights depending on your individual circumstances.

➤ *Fees* (annual management fees, commission charges for purchase of fund shares, etc.)

➤ *Portfolio turnover*—how often do the fund managers sell holdings and invest in others? If the fund manager buys and sells stocks in the fund frequently, that could mean higher expenses, around 3 1/2 to 3 3/4%, where many funds' expenses come in around 1 1/2 to 2%. Those expenses affect the fund's bottom line by 2%. Multiply 2% times 27 years (if the fund is in your retirement account) and you can see the effect of high turnover/high expenses on your investment.

➤ *Rating of the fund* by *Morningstar* (mainly for safety)

➤ Average *dividend income* as an annual percentage of overall fund growth—this helps me determine the fund's net performance. Most funds collect dividends from the stocks in their portfolios, then reinvest those dividends in more stock. The dividend income is counted as part of the fund's overall growth for the year. If too high a percentage of total returns is due to dividend income, then it's not the fund for me. For example, if a fund is up 10% for the year and 3% of that gain was dividend income, I probably would decide not to invest. Why pay a management fee for a net return of only 7% $(10 - 3 = 7)$, which I consider pretty mediocre performance?

With all the above information, I feel fairly well armed and informed, confident that I can compare the opportunities of one fund versus another. When in doubt, though, it's comforting to know that you can rely on *Morningstar*'s rating. After all, they are professionals at the rating game and do an excellent job in providing potential investors with timely, accurate information.

## Loaded Versus "No Load"

I believe investors should be wary of "back-end loaded" (12B-1) funds. These funds are sometimes sold as being "no-load" or "commission free" if you hold them through the penalty period (usually five full years). That's not completely accurate, however. Here's how it *really* works. In the same way a stockbroker gets paid to place a stock trade for you, the broker who sells you a particular mutual fund gets paid a commission, too, whether it's a loaded or back-end-loaded fund. In a loaded fund you pay an up front commission on the amount you invest. The amount of commission depends on the particular fund and the size of your investment.

But many investors feel paying a commission of around 5 to 6-1/2% up front is too much. They're afraid it will take too long for the fund to make enough money to justify the fees. So they look at 12B-1 funds, which do not charge a commission fee up front, right? But *somebody's* still got to pay the broker's commission for selling the fund. And that somebody is the fund itself. Here's the catch: the fund actually *borrows* the money to pay the commission to the selling broker. That money (and the interest on it) is paid back out of the fund's profits. So the interest cost of borrowing the money to pay broker commissions usually results in lower comparative yields than with a "loaded" fund.

There are two other problems with 12B-1 funds. First, many have higher management fees than front-loaded funds. These fees all come out of performance (portfolio) income. Second, the penalties for getting out of a 12B-1 fund before a full five years are very high. And according to industry statistics, most people stay in a mutual fund for only *three* years before selling. Not great odds for avoiding what can be significant penalties.

All funds are not created equal; many funds have high fees *and* can also subject holders to high penalties for early withdrawal. Being subjected to rear-end penalties is especially disturbing when the fund has declined in price due to poor investment performance. In this case, it is entirely possible that you could actually get back less money than you originally invested, even after several years invested in the fund. Again, make sure you read the prospectus to determine all the fees that are to be paid from income, so you will know what to expect. And remember, most mutual fund investment returns don't begin to approach what individual investors can achieve on their own with just a little bit of research and guidance.

# Closed-End Funds

Mutual fund investing provides two benefits to the average investor: professional management expertise, and greater diversification for smaller amounts of capital. The downsides are paying for that "professional" management through fees and penalties. However, there is one category of mutual fund that you can acquire for almost any amount of capital, and it will cost you only as much as you would pay for a stock trade (as little as $19.95 no matter how many shares you buy).

There are two broad types of mutual funds: *open-end* and *closed-end funds*. An open-end fund does not have a set number of shares; it can grow depending upon how many people want to buy in. All the mutual funds described above are open-end funds. A closed-end fund has a set number of shares, and—here's the important point—*it trades or lists on the NYSE just like stock in a company.* So you can buy shares in a closed-end mutual fund just like you would buy shares of Microsoft, or Ford Motor Company, or Du Pont. And rather than paying 4%, 7%, etc., in commissions to a mutual fund broker, you pay stockbrokerage commissions of just $19.95 per trade! And there are dozens and dozens of closed-end funds to choose from, all listed on the NYSE.

There's another great benefit to closed-end funds: *most of them trade at a discount to their net asset value.* For example, say the "Mellon Fund" is a closed-end fund trading on the NYSE. The portfolio of stocks owned by the Mellon Fund is worth $100 million. However, the shares of the Mellon fund itself might sell for only $80 million on the open market. **Most closed-end funds sell between 80 and 90% of their net asset value.** So if you want exposure to the mutual fund market and want more bang for your buck, why not look at some of the closed-end funds that are selling right now on the NYSE? Instead of paying a 5 or 6 or 7% front-end load, or a 4 or 5% rear-end penalty, why not buy shares for $19.95 a trade, whether you're investing $1,000 or $100,000?

If you choose to invest in a closed-end funds, make sure you avoid a new one. Why? Because as I said above, closed-end funds typically trade at a 10 to 20% discount to their net asset value. Generally within the first three months of a closed-end fund coming to market, it's automatically going to lose 10% of the value of its shares. So as long as you look only at closed-end funds which have been on the market longer than six months, and you want to put some of your investment money into mutual funds, closed-end funds are a great way to go.

# 7

# Treasuries and Zero Coupon Bonds

There is no real "secret" to investing in U. S. Treasury securities that you'll learn in this chapter, but there are some *derivative* securities on U. S. Treasuries that can help you plan your investment portfolio for the long term. Let's take a look at some facts about Treasury bonds and how they can be used to benefit the average investor.

U. S. Treasury bonds (or "T-bonds") are issued in minimum denominations of $5,000. They mature in anywhere from ten-plus years to 30 years (the 30-year bond is what is referred to as the "long bond" on the nightly newscast), and pay interest semi-annually. T-bonds can be purchased directly from the Federal Reserve through a Federal District Bank, or from any commercial bank or securities brokerage company.

# Zero Coupon Bonds

Many years ago, a few enterprising brokerage firms decided to begin trading in a derivative form of Treasury bonds. This derivative would pay no interest, but could be purchased at a deep discount to the bond's face value (maturity value). These new securities were called *strips*, because they were stripped of all interest payments but would become worth their face value on the maturity date many years hence. These securities are also referred to as *zero coupon bonds* because they obviously pay zero interest.

Strips, or zero coupon bonds, represent ownership of an actual bond that is held in trust by the issuing financial institution or brokerage firm. Many strips can sell for as little as $600 to $700, but will be worth $10,000 at maturity in 25 to 30 years. Strips give many people who could never afford it otherwise an opportunity to invest in an obligation that the U.S. Government must pay, one backed by its full-faith credit and taxing authority. Thus, they represent the ultimate safe investment.

There is another advantage to strips, or zero coupon bonds: they can be purchased in denominations of $1,000, rather than the $5,000 minimum on regular Treasury bonds. So an investor who contributes $2,000 annually to an Individual Retirement Account might be able to buy $10,000, $15,000 or $20,000 worth of bonds (due in 30 years) each year. Strips also provide an excellent planning tool for educational purposes and for retirement. Imagine the peace of mind for investors who know that in 30 years they will definitely have $15,000 or $20,000 coming due each and every year from Uncle Sam (a big boost to overall retirement income, for sure). These securities can help balance a portfolio in terms of risk over the long haul.

Zero coupon bonds are available for shorter-term periods, too—12, 13 14, or even 16 years. These securities can be quite useful in planning for future events like education, weddings, retirement, etc. They also make great gifts for educational purposes. Grandparents who invest just a few hundred dollars in a zero coupon bond can provide significant funds for their grandchildren's private school or college tuition. I've even heard of zero coupon bonds being used by businesses for promotional purposes. One automobile dealer gave away a $5,000 bond with each new car purchase. They also work well as incentives for employees who have provided outstanding service for their employers. For only a few hundred dollars an employer could give $5,000 bonuses to key employees, generating significant loyalty and goodwill in the process.

## Phantom Income

There is a drawback to these investments, though: *phantom income*. The IRS claims that even though an investor receives no interest payments on zero coupon bonds, each year the bonds are one year closer to maturity and (theoretically) worth that much more than the investor paid for them. (This is certainly not the case in real life, however.) According to the IRS, the yearly increase in value is taxable income. Investors must amortize the amount of the bond (in excess of what they paid for it) equally over the life of the bond, and pay taxes yearly on that amount.

For example, say you purchased a $10,000 zero coupon bond for $1,000, and the bond will mature in 30 years. Each year for 30 years, the IRS says you must pay taxes on a portion of the difference between what the bond is worth ($10,000) and what you paid for it ($1,000), or $9,000. That $9,000 is amortized, or spread out, over the 30-year life of the bond. $9,000 divided by 30 years equals $300, so every year you must add $300 to your taxable income on your income tax return.

There is a positive side to this IRS rule, however: when the bond matures in 30 years, there's no tax due on it. That $10,000 will be yours tax-free, to do whatever you want with it. For this reason, most people use zero coupon bonds in their IRA accounts. There, the bonds can mature without any tax liability, and the money is taxed at the regular tax rate only as it is withdrawn from the account after retirement.

Some strips or zero coupon bonds are marketed under different names by various brokerage firms. You may see them referred to as CATS (*C*ertificate o f *A*ccrual—*T*reasury *S*ecurities) or TIGRs (*T*reasury *I*nvestment *G*uaranteed *R*eceipts). Whatever they're called, they refer to zero coupon bonds on U.S. Treasury securities. Be aware, however: there are zero coupon bonds on other types of securities issued by other borrowers. There are also corporate zero coupon bonds, and municipal tax-free zeros. You must be very informed and cautious when selecting which securities to purchase. Make sure whatever bonds you purchase meet your investment needs and goals.

## Stocks Versus Bonds

I am a personal believer in the long-term benefits of owning stocks over bonds, with the exception of retirees who want to replace earned income with a constant flow of investment income. I usually recommend that investors use bonds *only* as a portfolio hedge when interest rates are high. Why? If you take any ten-year period over the last hundred years, the stock market has averaged a little over 12% growth per year. Naturally, there are peaks and valleys, but the overall yearly average is 12% growth. So if you are planning to be in the market for ten years or longer, why would you want to be in a bond or any other kind of investment if it pays less than 12% a year?

Now, there was actually a time—the 1980s—when bonds and CDs were paying double-digit interest. At that point, it made sense to use bonds and CDs to lock in those rates of return. And if in the future, we ever see an 11-year CD or bond that pays 13% interest, I'll be happy to invest in it. Why not, if I'd be getting double-digit returns on my money for no risk at all, other than the six-month penalty for getting out early? But unless inflation runs rampant, those kinds of interest rates are unlikely to happen again. And until they do, I believe that, based on historical record, you can get better rates of return by investing in stocks.

By the way, there are some equity investments—preferred stocks, for example—that act like bonds, paying increasingly higher dividend returns every year (in the case of some utilities, for example). And in Section IV, "Making Money in a Bear Market," you'll read about a type of corporate investment called a *convertible bond*, which has some of the advantages of both bond and stock ownership. But in general, unless you are preparing for imminent retirement or your risk tolerance is extremely low, I think most investors should stay in equity-type investments to maximize total returns over the longer term.

# Section II

# Stocks: The Basics

I believe that stocks are the easiest, most profitable means for investors to amass sizeable net worths in the shortest amount of time. Why do I advocate stock ownership so strongly? As I said in Chapter 7, **over nearly any ten-year period of time since the turn of the 20th century, stocks have dramatically outperformed fixed-income securities (bonds) by a significant margin.**

Stocks are the easiest vehicle for the beginning investor; with as little as $500 you can open a brokerage account and start trading. You can obtain information about companies and stocks on the Internet or TV any hour of the day or night. Unlike real estate, stocks are liquid, meaning you can buy and sell them whenever you want. Stocks are easy to understand, easy to trade, and with a little knowledge and application, easy to make a profit with.

But like most things in life, you need to put in some effort before you begin to trade stocks. You need to know the fundamentals. You must learn how to evaluate the company that is issuing the stock (after all, what a stock represents—and what you're buying—is actually a piece of a company). You must understand how not just value but *market perception* creates the price a stock sells for at any given time. You must learn a little about technical analysis: how to read the chart of a stock's past activity and then use it as a predictor of future price trends. Once you've mastered these areas, there are order strategies that will help you capture profits and limit your losses when you place your stock trades. And finally, you need to master the principle of margin: using someone else's money to reap greater profits from your investment dollars.

You may already be familiar with some of this information, but I encourage you to read it carefully anyway. Reviewing the basics is always intelligent when it comes to your finances. (How many of us forget the rule, "Spend less than you earn and invest the rest" whenever the holidays roll around?) More than that, however, I have included in these chapters my own criteria for choosing stocks successfully—what I look for in a company, which chart patterns I believe represent a great buying opportunity, which stop-loss orders to use and why, etc.

By reading these chapters, you can benefit from my 25-plus years of stock investing experience in bull and bear markets. After all, smart investors use other people's money (margin) to increase their profits on any given trade; why shouldn't smart investors use other people's experience to increase their profits and avoid expensive mistakes?

# Winning Wealth Strategies

# 8

# What to Look for in Stocks

There are some minimum guidelines that every investor should follow in deciding whether or not to buy a particular stock. Many of these guidelines are commonsense approaches to investing, and you may already be familiar with them—but do you *use* them when you invest? Far too many people lose money in the markets because they let their emotions get in the way of proper decision making. Following an established pattern of gathering criteria and analyzing the data carefully will help you stay out of trouble in the investment arena.

If you're going to invest in stocks it is always helpful to **know something about the company you are planning to invest in.** You should understand what the company does, what product or service it provides to generate revenue, and what its prospects are for future profitable operations. I like to look for several specific criteria that will help eliminate those stocks that aren't suitable candidates for my portfolio, so that I can concentrate on the ones that are.

Look AT:

## 1. Sales Growth

Once I select a company to evaluate and I understand what it does, perhaps the first thing I look for is sales growth. I want to invest in companies that have an historic track record of increases in sales every year. (I'd like to see sales growth of at least 10% year to year.) I also like to see consistent growth on a calendar quarter basis as well. I always compare one calendar quarter to the same calendar quarter of the previous year. This shows me actual sales growth without the seasonal fluctuation you might see in a retail company (which might show a growth spike right after the holiday buying season, for example) or a construction company (most of whose expenses might come in the spring building season).

## 2. Products and/or Services

I want to know what the company does in layman's terms (this is especially important for investments in computer and biotechnology stocks). What specific products or services does this company offer? Who are its customers and clients, and how strong is the customer base? Is this company in an industry notorious for slow collection of accounts receivable (any government contractor, for example)? How do its products compare with others available in the industry? Is this company a leader in its industry (like Microsoft, Intel, Nike, General Electric, etc.)?

If I don't understand what a company does or what product it manufactures, then I can't make an informed decision whether or not I want to be an owner. I need to know and understand how this company is going to make me money, and more important, when! Therefore, I must be thoroughly familiar with what the company does and how it operates.

## 3. Company Management

Back in 1978, Lee Iacocca took over Chrysler Corporation, an auto company close to bankruptcy.

As soon as Iacocca's hiring was announced, the stock's price jumped upwards. Well, I want my stock to jump, too, so I want to know about a company's management. I like to invest in companies that have strong, experienced management with proven track records of success. (Look at what Lou Gerstner did for IBM, or Jack Welch for GE.)

There are also companies I would never invest in *because* of their chief executives. Some CEOs are so poor at running companies that I know it's only a matter of time before the bottom falls out of the stock and I don't want to be left holding the bag. (I have chosen not to use any specific examples of these CEOs for obvious reasons.) I like to have faith that a company's management is seasoned and capable. After all, the CEO runs the company for the benefit of the stockholders who are its ultimate owners.

## 4. Balance Sheet

A strong balance sheet is needed to meet the continuing challenges of today's business environment, so I like to take a look at a company's cash on hand, as well as its ability to meet current indebtedness. For this reason, I look at two formulas: the current ratio (current assets to current debt) and total debt to equity. Remember the frenzied merger activity of the 1980s, when the buzzword was to "maximize shareholder value"? This usually meant that the company went heavily into debt, borrowing money to buy back outstanding shares of its stock at inflated prices. Then, to meet the increased costs of servicing the new debt, it would lay off thousands of talented, loyal workers in order to pare expenses. History tells me that a company with staggering debt can't and won't remain competitive in the long run, so I avoid companies with heavy debt-to-equity ratios.

## 5. Dividends

Although many high-quality companies don't pay dividends (choosing to reinvest the money in their own growth instead), I like to collect dividends whenever possible. Therefore, if I have a choice of two stocks in the same industry group, I try to select the one that pays dividends, all other things being equal.

## 6. P/E Ratio

I always look at the company's *price/earnings ratio*, or P/E—that's the ratio between what each share of stock earns divided by the current price of that share. (This is also referred to as the stock's *multiple*.) Looking at the P/E ratio will help you decide whether the price of the stock is high or low, when compared to the average P/E for its industry, and the market in general.

At the present time (2001) the average stock listed on the NYSE trades at about 25 times earnings. I look for stocks that are within these average ranges or less. A high P/E ratio can spell potential trouble for the long-term investor, because the price of the stock is not supported by the amount of earnings the company is taking in (although that is not always the case in high-tech stocks). I look at P/E very carefully for any of my buy and hold stocks, which are more long-term investments.

## 7. Technical Chart

I like to see if this is a good time to invest in the company by viewing the *chart* of its stock price. Charts (which are available on many financial Web sites and through most brokerages) give you a picture of the fluctuations in a stock's price over a particular period of time (days, weeks, months, years). The technical picture presented by the chart tells me if I am buying at a favorable time (remember, timing is everything in life) for this particular stock. This is not 100% foolproof, but evaluating a stock's chart definitely can be helpful in seeing the trends of growth or decline in a stock's price. You'll learn more about reading charts in Chapter 10.

## 8. Brokerage Recommendations

Whenever I'm looking at a stock, I review any brokerage research reports that may be available on the company. I like it when the stocks I select have been recommended by major brokerage firms for purchase by their clients. I also like to review the reasons why these analysts think it is a good time to buy this particular stock.

The stock and company information from these eight categories help keep me out of trouble, reasonably maximize my returns, and assist me in determining the right time to buy. If you use these criteria—along with whatever else you consider important—you will only strengthen your ability to maximize potential portfolio returns.

# 9

# Value Investing:
# Where's the *Real* Value?

In Chapter 8, we discussed doing our homework before determining how and when to buy a particular stock. But there are other elements to the decision making process that will give you a more well-rounded perspective of market and stock valuations.

It is fair to say that the financial markets are fickle in nature. If not, how else could you explain that today's $40 stock is *more* popular than when it was only $30 last week? There seem to be two distinct factors that actually influence decisions in stock market trading strategy. One involves finding stocks that have *real value* based on specific standards and accounting principles. (That is what we were looking at in Chapter 8.) The other is based solely upon *market perception* of that value—that is, how the stock might react in the short term to investor perceptions. I like to call this "perception versus reality."

It is actually the market's perception of a stock that induces its price to rise or fall. A stock may be worth the price it is selling for at the present level, but if investor perception of that stock is substantially different, the stock will likely move up or down accordingly. It may move up quickly in anticipation of an event that may not happen for years. (This is particularly true in the drug stock sector. An announcement of the discovery of an AIDS vaccine, for example, would likely move any stock's price up 50% or more no matter what the current price—even though the vaccine may not be marketed for years, if at all.) Or it may fall if the stock's earnings per share decline by as little as a penny.

The perception that the market has for value is often tainted, too. Sometimes stock valuations are much too excessive, leaving investors to wonder, "Who's doing all the buying at these price levels?" Other times, there may be stocks with truly good records of annual earnings increases for many years that are selling incredibly cheap. It is really the *market's perception* that an investor wants to gauge, and not necessarily the reality of investment value. After all, just like real estate, a stock is worth only what someone will pay for it.

There have been many instances of undervalued stocks that have been purchased for the long term by investors who have made fortunes as a result. Sir John Templeton and Warren Buffet are perhaps two of the best known value investors. They constantly search for the next opportunity that may yet be undiscovered by the rest of Wall Street. But **I generally like to look for stocks that are currently in an upswing, stocks where investor perception is high and getting higher so that I can ride the tide to even loftier levels.** Much, if not most, of my stock selection is based on *investor perception of market value* (which is often completely irrespective of basic corporate valuation methods) rather than actual value. I tend to look for stocks that have 1) shown price improvement and 2) seem to be perceived by investors as good values; then I ride the "coattails" on the influx of buying. I am a momentum investor at heart and like to take my profits quickly when trends seem ready to change.

I try not to be tempted with greatly undervalued but unpopular stocks. Instead, I look for stocks that are undervalued and just becoming popular. I will take the popular stock every time because it will usually maximize my short-term profit potential. Remember, stocks that are undervalued may be so for a reason, but until the perception on Wall Street changes in regard to that stock, its price will most likely continue to languish right where it is.

# 10

# Market Timing: Mastering Charts

I t's always interesting to me when someone says they want to invest in a stock because he or she heard from a friend it's supposed to rise 50% to 75% in the next year or so. If that's true, why not buy it right before it moves, rather than buy it now and hold it for an entire year? I find it rather strange that so many investors seem to want to put their money in a stock for an entire year to get a 50% return, for example, when they could get most of that—say 75% of the 50%—in a much shorter period of time.

When it comes to putting my money into any stock, I always ask, "*When* is this stock going to move, and *how much* of that movement can I capture on a timely basis?" For the answer, however, you have to take a look at what's called *technical analysis*, which helps you assess the timing of a stock's movement within the movement of the overall market.

As an investor, it's important for you to know when a stock is showing strength and when it is showing weakness. However, you can't always tell a stock's strength and weakness by looking at a Web site, CNBC, or the financial pages for that day's trading activity. To be certain of how a stock is performing relative to past history, it is necessary to examine a *chart* of the stock's activity.

Think of a chart as a picture of a stock's personality. It shows how a stock's price has risen and fallen in the past, thereby giving a fair indication of how it may react in the future under similar conditions. Using an analysis of this type of "technical" picture, you can identify certain trends exhibited by stocks that may lead to fairly accurate predications of future trading action.

Historically, technical evaluations are fairly accurate about 70% of the time. That means using this type of investment examination, you should be able to predict a stock's behavior with reasonable accuracy seven out of ten times—a pretty good percentage, to my mind. I use this type of technical evaluation myself (coupled with other evaluation methods) and find it to be accurate 70% to 80% of the time when used in conjunction with strong fundamental factors (as we discussed in Chapter 8).

# What to Look For

When we examine a stock's chart, we begin by looking for levels of obvious *support* and *resistance*. Take a look at the following chart, which shows the price of ABCD's stock, drawn as a graph progressing through time.

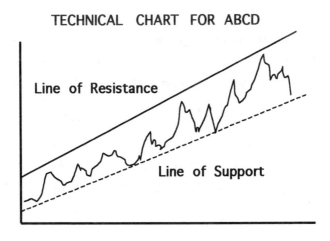

TECHNICAL  CHART  FOR  ABCD

Line of Resistance

Line of Support

You'll notice a dotted line drawn underneath the jagged line which represents the price of the stock. That lower line is called the "line of support." Whenever ABCD's stock price drops to a certain point, investors start to think, "Hey, this stock is a bargain!" So they start to buy ABCD stock, and the price starts to rise. That's the line of support: the price point where investors will support the stock's price and start buying.

On the other side of the stock price, there's another line called the "line of resistance." That's the point where investors start to feel that ABCD's stock is getting too expensive, so there are fewer people willing to buy at that price. At the same time, investors who already own ABCD don't believe the stock is going to go up much more, so they start selling their shares to take profits. The line of resistance represents the point beyond which people resist paying more for ABCD's stock.

The lines of support and resistance are fairly easy to identify on a stock's chart. Moreover, they can represent buying and selling points for the investor. When I look at the long-term picture of a stock, the lines of support and resistance can tell me if I'd be paying too much for a stock (if the price is above the line of resistance). Conversely, I can look at the line of support and see if the stock seems to be forming what's called a *basing pattern* at a certain price, in preparation for a large advance. Can you see how something as easy as looking at a stock's lines of support and resistance can help you decide when to buy?

## Classic Chart Patterns

A stock's chart can tell you much more than just the levels of support and resistance, however. There are certain classic patterns which you can observe in a stock's chart. These patterns have proven over many years, many stocks, and many different kinds of markets to be clear indicators of how a stock will move (up or down). With a little information, you will be able to spot these patterns in a stock's chart easily, and use them as indicators in making your investment decisions.

Take a look at the four patterns on the next page.

## GOOD PERFORMANCE

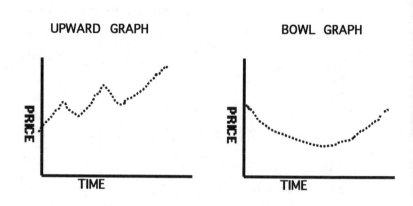

### UPWARD GRAPH

### BOWL GRAPH

## POOR PERFORMANCE

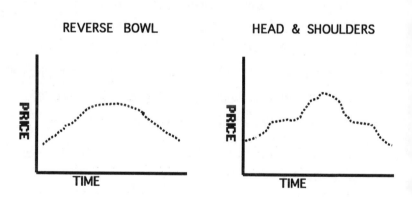

### REVERSE BOWL

### HEAD & SHOULDERS

I'm not going to discuss the Poor Performance graphs since it should be clear why you'd want to stay away from those stocks (unless you're selling short—see Chapter 22). It should also be obvious why the upward graph is considered good performance, since the stock's price is rising. But why would the bowl graph be considered good? Because most stocks don't move upwards over time to double in price, as is shown in the upward graph chart. Instead, the stock will usually stay at one level, then suddenly, over a period of 30 to 60 days, move substantially upward before leveling off again. That's a bowl graph pattern.

The bowl graph is one of my favorite patterns, because I want to *buy the stock as it moves up,* rather than buying and holding for a long period of time. With the bowl, I can see that this stock has started its upward movement, and I can get in on an already-established rise. True, I will only get 60% to 75% of the increase, but I will get that move in a very short period of time without having my money tied up during the long, flat period before the rise. I can play several stocks using the same investment capital over and over again, and get a collective return much greater than if I had purchased only one stock for the long haul.

**This is the essence of momentum investing.** When committing your capital, you must look for the "play of the day" and the "play of the week." You want to buy for short periods of time and get out quickly, thus maximizing profit potential to its utmost while still having the liquidity to invest in several opportunities in a short time span. Momentum investing requires diligent effort on your part. You must keep in close contact with your investments so that (if necessary) you can buy or sell quickly. No, you don't have to stay logged onto CNBC or Bloomberg 24 hours a day, but you will need to be available for consultation should your stockbroker call with fast-breaking information favorable to a profitable trade.

They say timing is everything in life. If that is indeed the case (and I believe it is), then you should be looking not only at fundamental investment strategies but also at indicators that help you to time your investments to maximize profits. Chart reading can be of valuable assistance in both these areas.

# 11

# Stock Terms: Language & Orders

There are a few order-entry strategies that can greatly assist you in protecting your profits and limiting your losses. There are also some stock terms you need to know to place your orders. Let's begin by reviewing the basics.

## The Bid and the Ask

To buy or sell a stock, you need to know the price it's currently trading, so you call your broker or check your online trading account to see the current price of the stock. What you'll see (or be told by your broker) are two prices: the *bid* and the *ask*. The bid is what you could currently sell the stock for if you owned it. The ask is how much you will pay if you want to buy the stock.

"But why aren't the two prices the same?" you may wonder. Because there's a *market maker* who's involved in every stock transaction. A market maker is an individual or company who specializes in trading this particular stock. In return for putting buyers and sellers together, the market maker receives a small amount on each transaction—the difference between the bid price and the ask price, which is called the *spread*. You don't really need to be concerned with the spread; you just need to know that when you ask for a quote your broker will give you two numbers, like this: "GE is at 47.75 by 48." The first price is the bid, the second is the ask.

## Market and Limit Orders

When you wish to buy or sell stocks, you place an order with a broker, saying, "Buy (or sell) so many shares of such-and-such stock." If you want to buy or sell the shares at their current price in the market, that's called a *market* order. If, on the other hand, you wish to buy or sell the shares at a *specific* price, that's called a *limit* order. Understanding the difference between market and limit orders is essential when it comes to the more sophisticated order-entry strategies in this chapter.

# Stop Loss Orders

Stop loss orders are designed to do exactly that: to stop you from losing large amounts in any given transaction. They can protect you from losses if the stock declines, or advances if you have "shorted" the stock, hoping it will go down. (We'll discuss selling short in Chapter 22.) If properly used, stop loss orders can also help you lock in profits for stocks that have increased in price, thus protecting you from profit erosion.

Stop loss orders are always placed *away from* (that is, different from) the current market price of a stock. There are two basic types of stop orders: *sell-stop* orders and *buy-stop* orders. We will only be dealing with sell-stop orders in this book because we'll be looking at situations where we own stocks and options that we're looking to 1) sell for profit or 2) sell to protect from loss.

# Sell-Stop Orders

**A sell-stop order is placed *below* the current market price.** It's designed to get you out of a stock when the stock declines to levels where you no longer want to be an owner. Since it is nearly impossible for you to keep watch over your portfolio all day every trading day, sell-stop orders can act as your ultimate protector, keeping you from incurring unnecessary losses when you aren't watching the stock.

Let me give you two examples of sell-stop orders at work.

## 1. Minimizing Your Losses if a Stock's Price Drops

Let's say you place an order with your broker to buy 1,000 "ABCD" shares at the market (meaning, at whatever price the shares are currently trading). The trade is executed at $15 a share. As soon as you buy the stock, you also place a sell-stop order at $13 a share. You make the order GTC (Good 'Til Canceled), so it will remain on the brokerage's books until it is executed or you cancel it.

A week later, you see on the news that ABCD is recalling millions of its widgets. You know this news will have a negative effect on ABCD's stock, so you call your broker immediately. He tells you ABCD's stock price dropped below $13 today, so your sell-stop order was triggered. You sold your shares at $12.50. (Why $12.50 when you placed the sell-stop at $13? With a sell-stop, as soon as the stock trades at or below that price, the order becomes a market order, and the stock sells at the current trading price. The price may be below the exact amount of the sell-stop order, depending on how fast the stock price is declining.)

You're not that happy about this transaction; after all, you just lost $2,500, or 16% of your original investment. However, that night when you look at ABCD's closing price, you discover the stock dropped all the way to $8. If you had not placed the sell-stop, you would have lost $7,000—almost 50% of your original investment! Do you see how effective sell-stops can be in helping you minimize losses in your portfolio?

One caveat about using sell-stops in this way: *you must allow for normal fluctuations in a stock's price.* Remember, stocks can trade in a fairly wide range every day, depending on market conditions, industry news, and individual investor interest. You don't want to be caught having sold a great stock just because its price dipped when the Fed Chairman hiccoughed (or some other relatively trivial and/or unrelated event).

A fairly safe way to determine the price point for your sell-stop order is to ask yourself, "How much am I willing to lose on this investment?" Every investment has the potential to provide you with either a gain or a loss. The secret is to decide just how much you're willing to lose, set your sell-stop, and then stick with that number unless the conditions of the stock change. (More about that in the next example.) And remember: if you end up selling your stock for a small loss and you still think the company is sound, you can always buy the stock back—at the lower price!

## 2. Locking in Gains if a Stock's Price Rises

Let's say those shares of ABCD you bought at $15 have now climbed to $20 per share. Your first thought might be to take your profits and run. But what if the stock climbs to $35 or $40 after you sell it at $20? Yes, you would have sold at a profit, but look how much more you missed out on.

Sell-stop orders can help you lock in profit while giving you the opportunity to hold onto the stock should it go up even more. How? By placing your sell-stop order *above* the price you originally paid for the stock but *below* the price it's currently trading. If you paid $15 and the stock is currently at $20, you could place a sell-stop at $18.50. If the price of the stock declines and you are "stopped out" at $18.50, you'll make less money than you would have than if you'd sold at $20, but you'll still make a profit of around $3.50 per share. And if the stock continues to rise to $35 or $40, you will be able to participate because you still own the shares. No matter what, you make a profit.

I make it a rule to check my stocks regularly, and if they are increasing in value, I adjust my sell-stop orders accordingly. That way, I lock in increasing amounts of profit without having to cut myself off from future benefits should the stock price continue to rise.

# Stop-Limit Orders—Avoid Them!

Remember at the beginning of this chapter, when I said there were two types of orders: market orders and limit orders? A market order instructs your broker to buy or sell the stock at the market, that is, at whatever price the stock is currently trading. A limit order, however, means you want to buy or sell that stock at a specific price—no higher or lower.

The same holds true of sell-stops. You can put in what's called a "stop-limit order," which can only be executed at your limit (the price you specify). Using the first example, if your $15 ABCD stock had dropped to $8 and you placed a stop-limit order for $13, you would not necessarily have sold it—unless it hit $13 on its way down.

Here's the problem with stop-limit orders: *stocks don't drop evenly*. ABCD could have gone straight from $14 to $12.50 and never hit $13. With a sell-stop order, as soon as the stock price drops to $13 or below, the sell order is triggered. With a stop-limit order, if the stock can't be sold for $13, the order doesn't happen, and you're stuck with the stock no matter how low the price goes.

Stop-limit orders can be dangerous in fast-moving markets and that's why I don't like to use them. I know many situations where great losses were incurred by investors trying to protect themselves from loss, only to have their protection rendered virtually useless because they used stop-limits rather than sell-stops.

One such example happened to a good friend of mine. (I wouldn't think of mentioning his name.) He had purchased a stock for $21 per share. The stock was a volatile one; it had been as high as $25 and as low as $5 during the previous several months. The company was well regarded in its industry, though, and was considered to be capable of rising into the $30 range when he bought it.

My friend placed a stop-limit order (obviously without consulting me) at $19 and pretty much forgot about his investment, feeling quite comfortable with his stop-limit order to "protect" him. The next week technology stocks as a group dropped dramatically. My friend's stock went from $19.50, to $19.23, to $18.85, before falling to $16 at the close of the trading day. But his stop-loss order was never executed because he had put a limit of $19 on the sale price, and the stock never hit $19 exactly.

My friend wasn't very clear on how stop-limit orders worked; he thought since the stock had dropped below the price he had set on his stop-loss order, his broker had sold the stock. He didn't bother to consult his broker about the status of his order until a couple of days later. Unfortunately, by then the stock was at $11 per share. At that point my friend (finally) called me and asked what he should do. After chastising him for not speaking with me sooner, I said, " If I were you I would sell now and take your losses, because I think that stock is headed even lower." He did, and I was right—the stock is now around $5 a share.

Had my friend used a sell-stop order instead of a stop-limit order, he would have been out of the stock somewhere in the $18-plus range. (I could say more about my friend's use of the stop-limit order, but I know he'll read this book.) However, the proper use of stop-loss orders can help you reduce downside damage to a portfolio in a falling market and maximize profits in a rising one.

# 12

# Using Margin to Increase Profits

Nearly every portfolio manager I know (except those managing mutual funds) uses some degree of leverage to increase profit potential. For individual investors, leverage usually takes the form of *margin*. Effective use of margin is extremely important in wealth building, because it provides much more buying power for every dollar of cash available for investment.

Margin is the *purchase of securities with cash and borrowed funds*. The securities themselves act as collateral for the loan, which is then repaid when the securities are sold (hopefully at a profit). The maximum margin percentage amount is controlled by the Federal Reserve Board. Many years ago the percent was established at 50%, where it remains today. That means if you have $10,000 cash in a brokerage account, you could borrow another

$10,000 from the brokerage, giving you a total "buying power" of $20,000 (or 200% of the cash amount you had available to invest). If you then used the whole $20,000 to purchase stocks, you would have 50% "equity" and 50% "margin debit" (the amount owed to the brokerage).

How can margin help increase your profits? Say you used that $20,000 to buy 1,000 shares at $20 each in M&N Corporation. You have $10,000 of your own money invested, plus $10,000 which the brokerage "loaned" you. A week later, M&N releases their quarterly earnings report. They did far better than Wall Street expected and as a result, the stock shot up to $25 a share. You decide to take your profits, and sell your 1,000 shares for a total of $25,000.

How much money went into your account when you sold your shares? $25,000. How much profit did you make on the sale? $5,000 ($25,000 − $20,000 = $5,000). But remember what I said earlier about margin: the money you borrowed from the brokerage firm has to be repaid when you sell the stock. So, you repay the brokerage its $10,000, leaving you with $15,000. But who gets to keep all the *profits* from that stock sale? **YOU**

**DO!** Instead of a 25% profit ($5,000 ÷ $20,000 = 25%), you made a 50% profit ($5,000 ÷ $10,000 = 50%). You essentially used money the brokerage loaned you to more than *double* the amount of profit you made.

That's the up side of using margin. However, there's a down side, too. I'm sure you've heard the term "margin call" as something that many investors fear. Here's why: by definition, when you borrow funds on margin to buy stock, the stock is considered collateral for the loan. Using the M&N example again, the $20,000 worth of M&N stock you bought was collateral for the $10,000 which the brokerage loaned you. As long as the stock keeps its value, there's no problem. But say there was some really bad news about M&N, and the stock dropped to $13 a share. The value of the collateral dropped from $20,000 to $13,000—which leaves you very little equity. So at this point (and perhaps long before) the brokerage would issue you a margin call. Either you would have to put additional cash into your account (or you could deposit more stock), or the M&N shares would be sold immediately at the current market value, to cover the difference between the value of the stock and the amount you borrowed on margin. Not a pleasant prospect!

Even with the possibility of margin calls, however, I believe that margin can be used in a prudent fashion. How? **Do *not* borrow to the maximum extent possible.** I usually counsel people to use no more than 25% in borrowed money when purchasing on margin. This amount will give you that added "boost" to your portfolio profits, but will keep you out of trouble should the overall market or your particular stock decline dramatically in value.

Margin, by itself, is a very useful tool if used diligently. Don't be afraid to use it to your advantage. Think of the many times you've had profitable trades that could have been enhanced by 25% or more using margin. If you do your homework on stock selection (following the guidelines in Chapter 8), margin can be an important ally in providing superior investment results. You should always consult with your financial advisor, though, to make certain that margin fits with your overall investment objective and your tolerance for risk.

# 13

# When to Take Profits—Or a Loss

One of the most difficult areas of effective portfolio management to teach is the psychology of investing. Everyone is willing to take a profit; however, few are willing to take a loss on their investments. We will even tend to hold losing positions for years, waiting for the prices to return to profitable levels before shedding the investments from their portfolio.

Our human psyche is so fragile at times that most of us refuse to recognize the symptoms of poor judgment. When we make a decision we make a decision, and that's it. Good, bad or indifferent, we've made a decision and we're going to stick to it. Sometimes this refusal to admit mistakes can be our downfall.

It may seem like a forbidden subject to some, but there is not a person alive who's been trading longer than three months who hasn't had a loss in something. Yet over centuries there have been dozens of examples of famous, successful men who have been victimized by their own inability to admit error. Call it ego, vanity, over-confidence or whatever: it is purely and simply a mistake to be that obstinate. None of us are infallible (although many of us think we are) and we all make decisions that we have regretted from time to time. The question is, how do we keep from making them? And how do we correct them when we do?

I'm going to use the example of what can happen in a stock portfolio to illustrate my point. Let's say you have purchased five different stocks at five different times over the last several months, and your portfolio is now fully invested (that is, if you started with $10,000 in cash, you have purchased $10,000 worth of stocks). News comes out regarding a stock that you have been watching for quite some time for an opportunity to buy. You feel the timing is right, but you don't have any "buying power" (no cash). So you decide that now may be a good time to sell some of your existing stock portfolio in order to buy into this new opportunity.

Looking at your portfolio and getting current quote information, you determine that your five stocks have the following profits and losses:

| | | |
|---|---|---|
| **Stock A** | $1,200 | profit |
| **Stock B** | – $900 | loss |
| **Stock C** | $2,300 | profit |
| **Stock D** | – $1,600 | loss |
| **Stock E** | $600 | profit |

You know you will need to sell at least two of your existing stocks to make your new purchase. If you're like most people, your first thought is that Stock A ($1,200 profit), C ($2,300 profit) or E ($600 profit) might be the best candidates. After all, you do have a profit in these stocks and even though they have been good investments, it may be time to take the profits and run. Of course, you would never dream of selling Stocks B or D because, after all, you have a loss in these stocks. It would be unthinkable to take a loss. These stocks will surely come back to the levels that you paid for them, and then (and only then) would you think about selling them. So you put in an order to sell Stocks A, C, and E because those represent the largest profits in your portfolio. *It's okay to take profits but not losses,* you think.

You now have just three stocks in your portfolio: B, D, and the new stock you purchased (we'll call it Stock F). As time goes by, F is holding at about the same price you paid for it, but the other two have continued their decline. Stock B now is worth $1,200 less than what you paid for it, and Stock D is worth $1,900 less. Your overall portfolio profits are being eroded because of your insistence of holding on to losers.

After several weeks, Stock F has performed well, showing a nice gain of $600. Stocks B and D, however, have continued their slide and now are worth a combined $4,000 less than what you paid for them. You are now in a position where your overall portfolio is only slightly ahead of the amount that you started investing with. You have been right on your stock selection in four out of six cases, yet your portfolio is only slightly ahead. In fact, after income taxes on the gains, you have an actual loss in terms of dollars.

It would have been far more sensible to have taken losses in the stocks that weren't performing well so you could take a position in Stock F. If you had kept your "winners" and sold your "losers," you could have created a tax loss benefit and still been able to buy Stock F. Your portfolio would be composed of four stocks (A, C, E, and F), all of which are "winners."

It sometimes pays very handsomely to accept small losses and get into something else. Keeping winners and selling losers has made more men rich than poor. It is an investment strategy used most effectively by Warren Buffet, whom I consider to be the premier securities investor of our time. It is also the best way to keep your tax liability as low as possible. Over the long run, you'll benefit nicely from this strategy if you refuse to allow your ego to get in the way of making intelligent business decisions. Remember, the stock you bought has no idea what you paid for it. It may never get back to the level that you paid. If you make a bad decision, *get rid of the stock.* Sometimes you have to take a step back in order to take two steps forward.

# When to Take Profits

I like to think about taking profits when I've made more money than I can ever spend. It hasn't happened yet, but it's fun to imagine. For the reader, though, I would advise taking profits *when the stock's situation has changed enough that you believe the stock is no longer a bargain at the present price level.* What I mean is, simply, that when a stock climbs significantly from the price you paid for it, you have to ask yourself if you would still want to buy it at these levels. If the answer is yes, then hold onto it. If the answer is otherwise, it could be time to sell.

When most people purchase a stock, they probably have in mind a preconceived price level at which they would be willing to sell. It may be significantly more than they paid for the stock, or it could be only modestly more. Whenever the stock reaches that sell point, however, the investor must watch it closely to see if it is going to continue to rise, or if it will decline due to selling pressure from others.

I like to use "sell-stop" orders (see Chapter 11, "Stock Terms") when my stocks reach the price levels I am looking to achieve. Sell-stop orders are placed at prices *below* the current price of the stock so that if a stock begins to drop back (thus eroding profits), the stock will be sold automatically to protect those profits. If the stock continues to rise, then you would continue to participate in those profits and simply increase the price of the sell-stop order to protect those additional profits as well.

Let's say I bought 1,000 shares of Stock F from the above example. I paid $20 per share, and I believe the stock's price will rise above $25 in the next month. I begin by setting a sell-stop order at $18. (This prevents me from taking any more than a $2 loss should the stock's price drop suddenly.) Within the week, however, I see my prediction about Stock F was correct: it has gone up to $22 a share. So I cancel my $18 sell-stop, and put in a new one at $21 (a little below where the stock is currently trading). The next day, Stock F is up again, to $24, so I put in a new sell-stop at $23. Thus, I have ensured a profit of at least $3 per share, while I can still continue to participate in the stock's rise in price. By the end of the month, Stock F is up to $27 a share. My current sell-stop is placed at $25, which was my original price target. No matter what, I'll make at least $5 per share.

Deciding when to take a profit can be nearly as difficult for some of us as taking a loss on occasion; therefore, we have to be ever mindful of the future growth prospects for our stocks at every price level. Stocks that go up tend to keep going up. Stocks that decline tend to do the same. We must keep an open mind when evaluating the current prospects for our investments by asking, "Would I buy the stock at this new price level?" If the answer is no, it could well be time to sell.

# When to Take a Loss

Let me make one thing perfectly clear: I *never* like to take losses. It doesn't mean that I don't do so, however. Taking a loss is always a psychological blow to the ego. But there is an old saying on Wall Street: "Your first loss is your best loss." I never could figure out how *any* loss would be a best loss until it happened to me, in what turned out to be a textbook example. As you will soon see, being able to decide quickly when to take a loss is important. Like most people, though, I prefer to think of taking profits, and try not to practice the art of being a good loser too often. Learning from my experiences, though, may help you decide whether or not to take a loss. (It should at least be entertaining!)

Several years ago I wanted to purchase call options on IBM stock and made the mistake of purchasing put options instead. (Don't ask me how; it just happened.) When I realized my mistake only a few minutes later, I had a paper loss of $2,700. "Unbelievable," I thought. "How could this happen to *me*?"

Well, sometimes mistakes happen, pure and simple. We're all human and we're all prone to make mistakes at times. I certainly didn't *want* to take a $2,700 loss in a period of about one hour, but after conferring with some of my colleagues— and I was really looking for sympathy more than information—we determined I should take the loss. Kicking and screaming, I did. And it was a good thing, too: if I had waited until the end of the day as I had planned, hoping that the stock would come back, I would have lost $16,000. Now *that* would have been a real "kick in the shorts."

I learned firsthand what is meant when someone says, "Your first loss is your best loss." Sometimes the stock you take the loss on never comes back. IBM did—although it took about three years for it to finally come back to where I would have bought it had the trade been done properly. I learned a substantial lesson that day, and I hope that you can learn from my example rather than from your own experience. (Learning from experience is nearly always more painful.) If your stocks aren't working for you, you need to sell them. There are plenty of good opportunities out there for you to take advantage of, rather than sitting with a portfolio of losers, waiting for them to come back somehow to profitability. I don't necessarily mean you should sell the same day that you buy (as I was forced to do). I simply want to impress upon you that if an investment isn't working *for* you, then it will probably eventually work *against* you. Get out of it and move on.

# Section III

# Momentum Investing

Now we move into some of my favorite investing strategies: momentum investing, mostly options-based trading. I like these strategies for several reasons:

➢ You can control large blocks of stock by investing a few dollars.

➢ In most momentum strategies, a small movement in a stock price has a magnified effect on the price of the corresponding option. Therefore, you have a greater potential for profit.

➢ You can receive very high rates of return on a monthy, instead of yearly, basis.

➢ You can make money whether the market goes up or down.

➢ You can buy and sell something you don't own and make money on it—legally!

Momentum investing may not be for everyone, but I believe that, with a little bit of study, these strategies can form an important part of your investment portfolio. But you do need to be smart. If momentum investing offers the opportunity for higher returns, these returns come at a higher risk. Therefore, I strongly suggest you study the strategies in this section thoroughly. Many people find it's best to pick one momentum strategy, get good at it, then learn another. Make sure you understand the underlying concepts and can figure out your potential risk of loss as well as your potential rate of return.

A couple of warnings. First, as I said in Chapter 3, momentum strategies are short-term investments, and require more attention than long-term buy and hold strategies. If you aren't willing to put in time on a daily basis to track your momentum investments, these strategies may not be for you. Second, start small. Set aside perhaps 10% of your investment capital to use on momentum strategies. Once you feel comfortable with your success rate, you can refer to the

Investment Allocation by Age table on page 34 to determine the proper mix of momentum and buy and hold investing in your overall portfolio. Third, especially at the beginning, invest only what you are willing to lose. Because options are more volatile than stocks, and because they have no underlying value (as we will discuss in Chapter 14), at some point you will undoubtedly lose money with these strategies. But based upon many years of personal experience (and profit), I believe the potential for success with momentum investing is great enough to make a few losses in the beginning worthwhile.

In this section you'll learn the basics of options (what they are, different kinds of stock options) and how you can make money buying and selling them. You'll also learn the very useful strategy of covered calls, and how you can earn a monthly income on stocks you already own. We'll cover more advanced options strategies like straddles, strangles, and spreads, which are all ways you can make money on a stock whether it goes up or down. Finally, we'll talk about the ways you can protect your portfolio from losses in the markets by the use of vehicles like index options.

# 14

# Fundamentals of Options

I always get a kick out of people who say they enjoy investing in stocks but would *never* touch the options market because it is too risky. Certainly the options market is risky, but isn't the stock market also? The biggest reason people lose money in the options market is simple: they try to use *stock* strategies for investing in the *options* market. You can't do that. You have to use option strategies in the options market. If you attempt to do otherwise, you are only inviting disaster.

I like the options market because of the leverage it gives: you can "control" a large number of shares of an expensive stock for only a few hundred dollars. But just as the leverage and potential for profit is enormous, so also is the potential for loss if you don't know what you're doing. By using the methods you will learn here, you can avoid the painful process of having to "learn by experience." You will have a strategy for entering and exiting the options market that you can use with confidence.

Let's start our options discussion by identifying and explaining some terms. (If you are not familiar with options trading or any of the terms discussed in this section, call any brokerage office and ask for the booklet, *Characteristics and Risks of Standardized Options*. It's published by the stock and options exchanges to inform potential clients about the options markets.)

## What Are Options?

Simply put, an option is a contract between two people, giving one the right to buy and the other the right to sell something of value at a specified price. You may be familiar with this kind of contract in real estate. For example, suppose you owned a house and wanted to sell it. You would put the house on the market for $300,000 and wait for a buyer. But suppose your co-worker Joe called you up and said, "Look, I'd like to buy your house, but I need some time before I do. So

I'd like to take out an option on your house. I'll pay you a small amount now—say, $5,000. In exchange, you'll sign a contract agreeing to sell me the house for $300,000 in three months. During that three months, you agree not to sell the house to anyone else. If by the end of three months I haven't come up with the money, my option will expire, you can put the house back on the market, and you'll be $5,000 richer."

In that case, you are selling Joe the right to buy your house for $300,000 within three months. What happens if Joe can't come up with the money or changes his mind? You keep the $5,000. What happens if he buys the house at the end of three months? You keep the $5,000 *and* you sell at the price you wanted ($300,000). You've made $5,000 more than you would have, just for holding onto the house for three months more.

What does Joe get from the deal? (More important, what would *you* get from the deal if you were Joe—that is, the person buying the option?) Joe basically "controls" the house for three months. You couldn't sell it to anyone else, even if the real estate market went way up or you found a buyer willing to pay double your asking price (not unless you bought back the option—more on that in Chapter 23, "Defensive Strategies"). By spending a mere $5,000, Joe gained financial power over an asset worth $300,000!

That's fundamentally how options work: you spend a small amount of money to gain control over the underlying property, whether it's a house, a stock, or whatever. Options are called *derivatives* because (unlike a piece of real estate or a stock) they have no inherent value. Instead, their value is derived from their control of the underlying property. Therefore, *the price of any option will change in accordance with any price change in the underlying financial instrument on which it is based.*

There are many different types of options: commodity futures options, index options, interest rate futures options, to name a few. However, here I'll discuss only stock options. Why? Because I believe trading in stock options are some of the easiest momentum strategies to understand and implement. I have used the techniques I discuss in this book for many years to make myself and others a great deal of money.

Not all stocks are *optionable*, meaning, not every stock traded on the financial exchanges will also have options trades on it. However, there are currently stock options on about 2,500 different companies available for trading—certainly enough to keep you fully invested if you want to be.

# Calls: The Right to Buy

There are two basic types of options: "calls" and "puts." A *call* gives the option buyer the right, but not the obligation, to purchase a certain stock at a specified price for a certain period of time. You could think of the option Joe bought on your house as a call option. The $5,000 he paid gave Joe the right, but not the obligation, to buy your house for $300,000 for a period of three months, right? In the same way, if you wanted to be able to buy 1,000 shares of "ABCD" stock at $50 per share but didn't have the $50,000 in your account at the moment, you could spend a small amount (say, $1 per share) to buy a call option on ABCD instead. That call would give you the right (but not the obligation) to buy 1,000 ABCD shares at $50 each for the next three weeks. By spending $1,000, you control

1,000 shares of ABCD stock for a certain period of time. Clear so far?

Now, let's go back to our house example. Joe has the right to buy your house for $300,000 anytime within a three-month period. But suppose a week after you sold Joe the option, your realtor calls. "Listen," she says, "I have a client who just got transferred here and needs a house fast. I drove her by your house and she loves it. She's willing to pay $325,000 right now."

"But I just sold Joe the option to buy my house for $300,000," you say. "What'll I do?"

"Buy that option back," your realtor tells you.

So you call Joe and say, "Hey, buddy, someone else wants to buy my house and quite honestly, it's a better deal." (Of course, you don't tell Joe how much the other person wants to pay for it.) "Can I buy that option back from you?"

"If the value of the house has gone up, the value of my option has gone up, too," Joe replies. "So you can buy back the option for $10,000."

What happened here? When the value of the underlying property (in this case, the house) goes up, *the value of the option goes up, too.* The same thing is true with stocks and calls. As the stock price moves up, the call increases in value as well, because the call owner has "locked in" the right to buy the stock at a specific price. Do you see why options go up and down in value based on what the underlying stock is selling for?

## Puts: The Right to Sell

Puts seem to give everyone problems at first, when it comes to understanding how they work, but it's actually pretty simple. A put is an option that gives the owner the right to *sell* a stock at a certain price for a specific period of time. A put holder (owner) locks in the price at which he wants to be able to sell the stock. Hopefully, that price will be higher than the stock is currently selling for in the open market. Puts can be very profitable in a bear market. If you know the expression "Buy low, sell high," think of puts as a way of being able to sell *high* when the stock price is *low*.

A put owner always hopes that the price of the stock will go *down.* As it goes down, the put option will be worth *more* money, because it gives the owner the right to sell the stock at a higher price than the stock is selling for in the open market. Say, for example, you own a put that gives you the right to sell 1,000 shares of XYZ stock at $40 each. One day XYZ takes a hit and drops to $30 a share. Because you own the put, you could sell XYZ shares for $40 each in the open market. (The Options Clearing Corporation, or OCC, would randomly assign your sale to whoever sold a put with the same strike price as yours [$40].) At the time of the sale, your put option would be worth at least $10,000 (the difference between $40 and $30, or $10, times 1,000 shares).

Calls and puts are two sides of the same coin. A call option gives the owner the right to *buy* something; a put option gives the owner the right to *sell* something. When we own puts, we hope the stock price goes *down.* When we own calls, we hope that the stock price goes *up.* It's simple!

# Contracts

Option "contracts" are sold in denominations of 100 shares, meaning that one (1) contract of an option represents 100 shares of stock. Therefore, ten (10) contracts would represent 1,000 shares. Each contract may sell for only $100 or $200, but will represent 100 shares of a stock selling for, perhaps, $50 or $60 per share. So for only a few hundred dollars, you can control stock worth several thousand dollars, by owning an option on that particular stock.

# Expiration Date

Unlike stocks, options have *expiration dates*. This is why many people feel options are risky: if you hold options too long, they expire and become worthless. We have to be nimble when trading options, and aware of how quickly an anticipated move in the stock price will occur. Options trading is not for the faint at heart, but much of the risk can be eliminated by using the strategies and techniques discussed in this book.

Technically, all stock options expire on *the Saturday following the third Friday of the expiration month.* An option for October 2001 would expire October 20th, since that's the Saturday following the third Friday. Truthfully, we really don't care when our options expire, but we *do* care about the last day we can trade them, which is the *third Friday of the month.* So for all intents and purposes, options expire on the third Friday. If we don't sell them by that time, we're out of luck.

# Strike Price

The *strike price* of an option is the price at which you have the right to exercise the option—that is, to buy or sell the stock. Remember, options give us the right but not the obligation to buy or sell a certain stock at a specific price. That price is the strike price. If you wanted to purchase an option to be able to buy or sell XYZ stock at $35, for example, your strike price would be $35.

Strike prices go up in predetermined increments, with the minimum strike price being $5 per share. For stocks trading at less than $25, strike prices move in increments of $2.50, so there would be a $5 strike price, a $7.50, $10, $12.50, $15, and so on, up to $25. For stocks priced from $25 to

$200, strike prices rise in increments of $5 ($25, $30, $35, $40, etc.). Over $200, the increments increase to $10 ($210, $220, $230, etc.).

There are three important terms when it comes to an option's strike price: *in the money, at the money,* and *out of the money.* They refer to the relationship of the strike price to the price where the stock is currently trading. Remember how ABCD was trading at $50 a share? You wanted to own it but you didn't have the capital to buy the shares, so you bought a call option instead. You paid $1 a share to buy a call option that gave you the right to buy 1,000 ABCD shares at $50 each. ABCD is trading at $50, and your call had a strike price of $50 a share. There's no difference in those two prices, is there? ABCD's strike price is *at the money*—meaning the strike price and the current trading price of the stock are the same. All you're buying when you purchase this call option is *time*; you have the right to buy ABCD stock at $50 a share (where it's trading right now) for however many days until the option expires.

Now, suppose you wanted to buy ABCD stock but didn't want to pay $50 a share. You could buy a call option that would give you the right to buy

ABCD at $45 a share instead. (Yes, they sell those kinds of options.) But those $45 call options would be more expensive. Why? When you buy the ABCD call option with a strike price of $45, that means you can buy the stock for *less* than it's currently trading. When a strike price is *below* the current price of the underlying stock, it's said to be *in the money.*

As you'll see in the next chapter, however, we don't just buy and sell options when we want to purchase the underlying stock. Most of the time, we buy options in order to sell them at a profit before they expire. We usually wish to buy call options with a strike price *above* the stock's current trading price—or *out of the money.*

Why would we want to do this? Because *options with a strike price that's out of the money cost less.* For example, if ABCD's stock is at $50 a share, the "at the money" options (with a strike price of $50) might cost you $1.50 each, but the "out of the money" options (with a strike price of $55) might be $0.50 each. You could purchase the same number of contracts for much less money. If the price of the stock rises, the value of both the $50 and the $55 options will go up, but you would have paid a lot less money for the options with the higher strike price. (Conversely, if the stock is trading at $50, the $45 options mentioned above would be trading for at least $5 "in the money" value, plus some time value, too.) By buying options at an "out of the money" strike price, you could make a greater percentage profit on a smaller investment. (When using put options, the terms *in the money* and *out of the money* are reversed. Please see the Glossary for a simple explanation.)

If this seems a little complicated, don't worry. It's only important if you wish to understand why options are priced the way they are. *In the money, at the money,* and *out of the money* are also terms a broker will use when giving you options quotes. You'll hear more about these terms throughout the rest of Section III.

# Where to Find Options Info

If you've ever followed a particular stock, you already know that it has a *stock symbol*—letters that represent that company's stock on the exchange where it's traded. (If you don't know the stock symbol for a particular company, you can look it up on the Internet.) Stocks listed on either the New York Stock Exchange (NYSE) or the American Stock Exchange (ASE) will have one-, two- or three-letter designations. IBM, GE (General Electric), MCD (McDonald's), IP (International Paper), are examples of stocks trading on the NYSE. Stocks traded on the Nasdaq or over the counter (see Glossary) will have four or more letters representing the company name: INTL (Intel) and YHOO (Yahoo) trade on the Nasdaq. If you don't know a company's symbol, just go online to sites like "Quicken.com," or the financial sites of Internet services like AOL, Yahoo, MSN, etc. Or you can call your stockbroker for assistance. I'm sure he or she will be glad to help.

Just like stocks, options are listed on exchanges such as the Chicago Board of Options Exchange (CBOE). You can check options prices daily in any financial newspaper. The same stock symbols are used on the options exchanges, so if you want to see if a particular company is optionable, you can look for their symbol on the financial pages of major newspapers like the *Wall Street Journal* and *Investor's Business Daily*.

# 15

# How Options Trading Works

O ptions trading can seem filled with pitfalls for the unwary or inexperienced investor. But with a little background and a little understanding of options trading strategies (which are different than stock trading strategies, as we said in the last chapter), options trades can be a very profitable source of cash flow in your portfolio.

Let's review an example of exactly how options trading works. We'll start with a fictitious company, "XYZ" (that's its stock symbol). As we said in the last chapter, both the put and the call on XYZ stock would expire on the same day of the month indicated. So if you wanted to look at options expiring in September, they'd be listed as "XYZ September ____ (p)ut or (c)all." The "_____"is the *strike price* of the option. (Remember, this is the price at which you have the right to exercise the option—that is, to buy or sell the stock. If you wanted to purchase an option to be able to buy or sell XYZ stock at $35, for example, $35 would be the strike price.)

Say it's late August and XYZ is currently trading at $35 a share, but you believe the stock is going to increase in value. Therefore, you want to buy a call, which will give you the right (but not the obligation) to *buy* XYZ stock at $35 per share. You're going to spend a small amount of money to lock in that stock price for a certain period of time (until the option expires on the third Friday of the month). So you open the financial pages, turn to the listings for the options exchanges, and see what the XYZ September calls are going for.

But here's the truth about options: **we rarely if ever buy an option to exercise it**—that is, to buy the stock. (There are some specific strategies that do require us to buy the stock, but I'll address those strategies in Chapter 16, "Covered Calls.") Nearly always, we simply buy the option to sell it—at a profit—to someone else before it expires.

Here's how it works. Say you bought a September 35 call option on XYZ stock. That meant you have the right to buy XYZ's stock for $35 a share. But what happens if the stock price goes up to $40 a share? You still have the right to buy the stock at $35—$5 less than the open market. Do you think there might be someone who would like to buy that option from you? More important, do you think your option will be worth *more* than when you bought it originally, when the stock was trading at $35? *Your option is now worth at least $5 more than when you bought it, simply because the price of the stock has gone up.* Instead of putting a whole lot of money into XYZ stock (and tying up your capital), you can make exactly the same dollar amount of profit per share by buying and selling the option as you would have by buying and selling the stock!

We never buy options to exercise them (to actually purchase the underlying stock); we only buy options to turn around and sell them to someone else for a profit. We don't have to worry about to whom we're going to sell our options. There is a ready and liquid market for options, regulated by the exchange the option is listed on, like the CBOE or AMEX, etc.

To review: if you feel a particular stock is going to go *up*, you would buy a call option. If you feel a stock's price is going *down*, however, you would buy a put option. Owning puts gives you the right, but not the obligation, to sell a particular stock at a particular price. Say you didn't like the way ABC's financials were looking, and you thought their stock price (currently $20 per share) was going to take a dive after the next quarterly earnings report. You would buy the ABC September 20 puts, which give you the right to sell a certain number of shares of ABC stock for $20 each.

Now, say you were correct: the first week of September, ABC announced disappointing quarterly earnings, and the stock price dropped to $17. Do you think your put option—which gives you the right to sell the stock at $20 instead of $17—would be more valuable than when you bought it? You bet! So now you can sell that put option to someone for at least $3 more than when you bought it ($20 − $17 = $3). The stock price went down and yet you made a profit!

# Choosing Your Options

You may be saying, "Okay, Chuck, that makes sense—but how do I know *which* options to choose? And at what strike price?" Here are a few examples that should help you. Let's start with call options, specifically with XYZ. (Remember, this is the company whose stock you think is going to rise in value.) The first thing to do is take a look at the history of the price of XYZ stock. You check the charts (see Chapter 10) and discover XYZ has traded at various levels over the near term (between $32 and $47 per share) and is currently at $37. (It's gone up since our last example!) You call your stockbroker and say, "Tom, what are the call option prices on XYZ for strike prices close to $37, where XYZ is trading today?"

"Let me check," says Tom, and he looks up the prices on his computer. Then he quotes you the following prices of some options on XYZ's stock:

| | |
|---|---|
| **September 35 Calls** | $ 3 1/2 |
| **September 40 Calls** | $ 1 1/2 |
| **September 45 Calls** | $ 3/8 |

(While stocks are now quoted in dollars and cents, options are quoted in fractions until June 2001. After that point, options are also slated to convert gradually to trading in dollars and cents.)

Let's go over each component of the quotes Tom gave you. September is the month in which these options expire. (Remember, options always expire the Saturday following the third Friday of the month, so if these options were for September 2001, the last day you could trade them would be Friday, September 21st.) The numbers immediately following (35, 40, 45) are the strike prices for these options, or the price at which you would be able to buy or sell the stock (depending on the kind of option). "Call" means the kind of option: you are purchasing the right to buy the stock.

Remember, each option contract is for 100 shares of stock. To figure out how much money you'll be spending, you must multiply the price of the option by 100. So for one (1) contract (100 shares), your investment would really be $350 ($3 1/2 x 100) for the September 35 calls. For the September 40 calls it would be $150 ($1 1/2 x 100). The September 45 calls would be $37.50 ($3/8 or 0.375 x 100).

Now, whenever you invest in options, you have a choice of scenarios and strategies. There is no right or wrong strategy, but some will be more profitable than others. Since you want to make as much profit as possible, let's look at ways to accomplish this using the above prices. If you had a limited amount of money to invest—around $1,000—you could invest it in one of the following ways.

1. You could buy three (3) of the September 35 call option contracts, thereby "controlling" 300 shares of stock.

2. You could buy six (6) contracts of the September 40 calls, representing 600 shares.

3. You could buy 26 of the September 45 contracts, controlling 2,600 shares.

More is not always better in the options market, but if this stock does what you expect it to, let's see how much money you could make on a $1,000 investment using these three scenarios.

Suppose XYZ's stock performs as you had hoped. Two days later you check the stock price and it's at $39 per share, up $2 from where it was when you bought the options. Excited, you check the option prices, which are now as follows:

**September 35 Calls**     $   5
**September 40 Calls**     $ 2 1/4
**September 45 Calls**     $   5/8

Let's take a look at your three scenarios. If you had used your $1,000 to purchase the September 35 calls—remember, you would have bought three contracts at $350 each—those three contracts are now worth $500 each. You made $450 in just two days ($500 − $350 = $150; $150 x 3 = $450), or a 43% profit. (To figure your profit percentage, you divide your profit [$450] by the amount you paid [$1050].)

But let's take a look at the other two choices. If you bought the September 40 calls, you would have paid $150 for each contract, and you bought six contracts for a total investment of $900. Those calls are now worth $2.25 per share, or $225 per contract. (Remember, a contract represents 100 shares of stock.) You have six contracts, so your call options are now worth $1,350. Your profit is

$450—the same as in the first example. But wait! You paid *less* for those September 45 calls, didn't you? Your total investment was $900. To figure your profit percentage, divide your profits ($450) by your total investment ($900). Your profit percentage on this trade is 50%.

What about your last choice, the September 45 calls? You would have paid $37.50 per contract for 26 contracts, for a total investment of $975. Those contracts are now worth $62.50 each ($5/8 is $0.625, multiplied by 100), so you receive $1,625 when you sell your 26 contracts ($62.50 x 26 = $1,625). Your profit per contract is $25 ($62.50 – $37.50 = $25), times 26 contracts, for a total profit of $650—more than the other two choices. Your profit percentage is $650 divided by $975, or 66%!

Let's look at the returns for these three scenarios in chart form. (Please note: calculations for these returns do not include commission charges, if any.)

## Scenario 1

| | |
|---|---|
| Option: | September 35 calls |
| Buying price: | $3 1/2 per share ($3.50) |
| Total bought: | 3 contracts (300 shares) |
| Total investment: | $1,050 (300 x $3.50) |

| | |
|---|---|
| Selling price: | $5 per share |
| Total sold: | 3 contracts (300 shares) |
| Total received: | $1,500 (300 x $5) |
| Profit: | $450 ($1,500 – $1,050) |
| **Total return:** | **43 % ($450 ÷ $1,050)** |

## Scenario 2

| | |
|---|---|
| Option: | September 40 calls |
| Buying price: | $1 1/2 per share ($1.50) |
| Total bought: | 6 contracts (600 shares) |
| Total investment: | $900 (600 x $1.50) |

| | |
|---|---|
| Selling price: | $2 1/4 per share ($2.25) |
| Total sold: | 6 contracts (600 shares) |
| Total received: | $1,350 (600 x $2.25) |
| Profit: | $450 ($1,350 – $900) |
| **Total return:** | **50 % ($450 ÷ $900)** |

**Scenario 3**

| | |
|---|---|
| Option: | September 45 calls |
| Buying price: | $3/8 per share ($0.375) |
| Total bought: | 26 contracts (2600 shares) |
| Total investment: | $975 (2600 x $0.375) |
| | |
| Selling price: | $5/8 per share ($0.625) |
| Total sold: | 26 contracts (2600 shares) |
| Total received: | $1,625 (2600 x $0.625) |
| Profit: | $650 ($1,625 – $975) |
| **Total return:** | **66% ($650 ÷ $975)** |

In terms of percentage, the $45 calls made the largest gain, increasing about 66% in value. The $40 calls increased about 50% in value, and the $35 calls were up about 43%. You get more "bang for the buck" in terms of percentage price movement in the option that is *above* the current price of the stock (out of the money calls) rather than those that are at or near the price of the stock. This will nearly always be true.

You can see by this chart the power that leverage has in the total return potential on a portfolio. It is for this reason that I believe a strong understanding of the options market and judicious use of options trading can enhance your overall investment profitability.

# 16

# Covered Calls

In this chapter we will learn about the exciting strategy of writing covered calls. (Don't be concerned if you are not immediately familiar with this term. We will cover everything you need to know to employ this strategy successfully.) Covered calls are a way of generating monthly income from a portfolio of stocks by selling options on those stocks. Income is generated by the option premiums you receive.

In the last chapter, you learned about buying and selling options. Just as you would with a stock, you went to the financial pages or your broker, you found a particular option you wanted to buy and purchased the option. Your goal was for the price of the option to go up so you could sell at a profit, right? Fairly simple. But there is another way you can use options to generate profit: if you own stock, you can sell someone the option to buy that stock from you at a set price. Did you buy an option? No. You are basically creating something out of thin air—the right to buy your stock—and selling it to someone who considers it to be of value. Amazing, isn't it?

To put this strategy in perspective, you must understand a fundamental truth about investing: **in the U.S. securities markets it is quite legal to sell something that you do not own.** Did you own the option on your stock because you bought it? No—but it's completely legal for you to sell an option on your stock. You are essentially selling something that you did not "own." You couldn't do this in every financial market around the world, but here in the U. S., it's a very common occurrence among savvy investors. Selling something they do not own is done every day by thousands of people in the stock and options market. Now, certain rules must be followed so the process stays legally compliant and manageable. But once you know and understand those rules, strategies such as covered calls can be very exciting, convenient and profitable.

# What's a Covered Call?

In a covered call, you are giving someone else the opportunity to buy your stock from you (usually at a higher price than you paid for it). This is accomplished by selling them an option to purchase your stock. The process of selling options that you do *not* "own" (since you didn't buy them), on stock that you *do* own is referred to as *writing*. Writing is, simply, selling an option that you do not currently own. (If we did own it, we would simply be selling the option, not writing it. Think of writing as creating an option that was not in your portfolio before.)

The second term is the word *covered*. Remember I said that this strategy was designed to generate income by selling options on stocks you already own? When you write an option, you give someone the right to purchase your stock. But you also create an *obligation* for you to hold on to the stock and deliver it for sale, should the buyer of the option want to purchase it. When you own the underlying stock on which you sell an option, your obligation to deliver the stock is said to be "covered." (Think of it in the same way as having enough money to "cover" your bills or a bet. If you sell someone an option to buy stock from you, you need to have enough stock to "cover" that promise.)

The last term is *calls*. As we discussed in Chapter 14, a call represents the right to buy a stock at a specific price for a certain period of time. In writing covered calls, you will be dealing with call options only. So, this process of purchasing (or owning) stocks and writing options on them is referred to as "writing covered calls." Some stockbrokers also refer to this strategy as a "buy-write," but it's exactly the same process.

# The Purpose of Covered Calls

The reason that we use covered calls is to *generate an income*. When we sell something we get paid for it; and when we sell an option, we get paid for it, too. Therefore, when we sell someone else the right to buy our stocks from us, they pay us a fee, called an option "premium," for that right. (They must, however, decide to buy the stock by the option expiration date.)

To help you master this, let's go back to our real estate example. Suppose you bought an apartment building as an investment, hoping that it would increase in value over the years that you intend to hold it. But how could you generate an income from that investment to pay maintenance bills, utilities, real estate taxes, etc.? The answer would be to rent out the apartment units to generate a *monthly income* to cover the expenses of owning the apartment building.

**Think of the process of writing covered calls as monthly rental income on your stocks.** Owning a portfolio of growth stocks is great, but unless you sell some of those stocks on a monthly basis, you generate virtually no income from your portfolio. By writing covered calls on your stocks, it's possible to generate a monthly income while waiting for your portfolio to increase in value.

With covered calls, you have the potential to generate profit in two ways. First, when you sell the option, the money you receive is pure profit, since you yourself are writing the option. (Remember, we said that when you write an option you are creating it from thin air; it's not something you bought from anyone else.) But when you sell a call option, you are giving someone else the right to buy your stock from you at the price that you agreed to sell it (the option strike price). But who decides the strike price? *You do.* Now, what strike price do you think you should choose: one that's below, the same, or above the price you paid for the stock? In most circumstances, wouldn't you want to get *more* money, should the person who bought the call option decided to execute it? By choosing a strike price *above* the price you paid for your stock, you are giving someone the right to buy your stock from you at a profit. If the buyer exercises the options you wrote, you end up selling your stocks at a higher price than you paid for them. So you make money selling the option, and you make money selling the stock—two possible sources of income. This is the essence of writing covered calls.

Now, by this time you may have several questions, like, "Who do I sell my options to?" or, "Who would buy my stock for more than I paid for it?" or something of that nature. My answer is "Who cares?" There are hundreds of thousands of investors every month who use this strategy to supplement their income. I use it, too, on occasion, for income and to offset downside risk in my portfolio.

To answer the question about who purchases these options, refer back to Chapter 14, where you learned about options exchanges like the CBOE (Chicago Board of Options Exchange). The exchange matches buyers and sellers to execute orders. There are plenty of buyers out there for your options, and it's your stockbroker's responsibility to place the order for you so that your order will be executed. As to who buys the option or the stock, we never know who, and *we do not care*. We only know that if our stock rises substantially above the option strike price, someone will buy it, giving us a nice profit.

# Covered Calls: Example #1

Let's see how effective covered calls can be in generating cash flow. Say you owned 1,000 shares of ABCD stock, which you purchased for $18 a share. When you purchased the stock six months ago, you felt that it had prospects of rising to about $25. Since then, though, it has done virtually nothing and its prospects don't look that great. You would be happy to sell it for just about any price above what you paid for it.

At this point, you may want to consider writing a covered call on the stock to generate some income and to offset the fact that the stock has done nothing for you for six months. So you call your stockbroker to get a market quote on the available options on this stock.

(That reminds me of something else you should know about options: not every strike price will have an available option. If your ABCD stock is currently selling for $18, do you think there would be anyone out there who would want to buy an option that would give them the right to buy your stock at, say, $50 a share? Probably not. That's why you need to check with your stockbroker to see what options at which strike prices are currently available, i.e., being bought and sold. Usually there will be options within a fairly narrow range above and below the price where the stock is currently trading.)

As ABCD is currently trading at $18, you know that there are options trading at strike prices of $17.50, $20 and $22.50. (Remember, for stocks valued below $25, strike prices go up in increments of $2.50.) So you ask your broker for the quotes on these options expiring this month (March). He gives you the following market quotes. (Remember, a stockbroker will always quote you the *bid*—the price where you could sell the option—and the *ask*—the price you would buy the option. Since you're planning to write [sell] the option, you're interested in the bid side.)

|  | Bid |  | Ask |
|---|---|---|---|
| **ABCD March 17.50 calls** | 1 | x | 1 3/8 |
| **ABCD March 20 calls** | 1/2 | x | 3/4 |
| **ABCD March 22.50 calls** | 1/16 | x | 1/4 |

After examining these market quotes, you quickly dismiss the March 22.50 calls because they would bring in only $62.50 in total income (1/16 times 10 contracts, or 1,000 shares of stock—1 contract equals 100 shares, remember). Also, the March 17.50 calls would require you to sell the stock for less than it is currently selling for and even less than what you paid for it.

That leaves the March 20 calls. In examining them, you find that you could gain $500 by selling the right to purchase your stock for $20 per share. You could write ten (10) contracts of the March 20 calls at a bid price of $1/2 each ($1/2, or $0.50, times 10 contracts, or 1,0000 shares) for a total profit of $500 (minus commissions). By doing this, you would generate an immediate income of around $500. Since you paid $18,000 for the stock ($18/share x 1,000 shares), by generating an income of $500 you have created an investment yield of 2.7% ($500 ÷ $18,000 = 2.7%). If you had done that each and every month for the six months you have owned the stock, you conceivably could have generated a 16.6% return on your investment.

But that's only half the story. Say the week after you write the covered call, ABCD's stock rises in price to $21.50. Whoever bought the call option on your stock will exercise his or her right to buy your shares for $20 each—and you will have locked in a capital gain of $2 per share, or $2,000 total. This $2,000, when added to the $500 you previously received, gives you a total income of $2,500. This now represents a powerful 13.9% return for the month! Even though you had to sell the stock at less than full market value, your return is still very respectable.

As you can see, when writing covered calls you must be willing to limit your ability to profit from potential growth in a stock's price. But remember this: if the stock doesn't go up in price, or doesn't rise beyond the strike price of the option, will the person who bought the option exercise it? Probably not, since he or she can buy the stock for less money on the open market. So the options would simply expire, and those 1,000 shares of ABCD stay in your portfolio—and you've made $500 even though they didn't go up in value. And here's the best part: you can write another covered call on those same shares next month! Do you see how you can continue to use this strategy every month to produce notable results, i.e., cash flow, into your portfolio?

# Covered Calls: Example #2

Now, let's say you are thinking of the best way to invest $10,000 to maximize your income and to allow for some growth in your stock portfolio, too. You discuss this idea with your stockbroker and he suggests that you purchase "XYZA" stock that is selling at about $9 per share. He tells you that XYZA is a growing company and the stock has been as high as $15 this year and as low as $7. XYZA has options trading on its stock, and your broker gives you the current option prices as follows:

|                      | Bid |   | Ask   |
|----------------------|-----|---|-------|
| **XYZA March 10 calls**    | 1   | x | 1 3/8 |
| **XYZA March 12.50 calls** | 1/2 | x | 3/4   |

Now, before you purchase any stock, there are several things you should know about the company (as we discussed in Section II, "Stocks: The Basics"). However, in this case, let's assume that XYZA meets your investment criteria. You are now ready to invest your money if you can get a good return on your investment.

Let's assume that you would be willing to purchase 1,000 shares of XYZA stock at $9 per share, or $9,000. But instead of simply purchasing the stock, what if you were to purchase it and *at the same time* write a call option on those shares? (Yes, you can do that—it's completely legal.) With 1,000 shares purchased at $9 each, you could write 10 contracts of either the $10 or $12.50 calls and get an immediate return on your investment.

Let's examine which choice gives you the best total return. By writing the XYZA March 10 calls, your option premium income would be $1,000 (10 contracts times the $1 bid price of the option, or $1,000). To figure out your current yield on the investment, you would divide your profit ($1,000) by the amount you invested ($9,000), which is 11.1% (1,000 ÷ 9,000 = 11.1%). Assuming you sell the option the same day you buy the stock, you will have made an 11% profit immediately.

But wait—if the stock rises above $10 per share and the option you sold is exercised, you will also have a capital gain of $1,000. (The capital gain computed by subtracting the price you paid for the stock [$9] from the strike price of the option you wrote [$10].) Add that to the original $1,000 option premium income, and you find this transaction has the potential to provide a $2,000 profit, or a 22.2% total return.

Before making your decision, however, you need to examine the opportunities presented by the other choice, the March 12.50 calls. These would bring an income of $500 when sold at the bid price of $1/2, for a 5.5% investment yield. ($1/2 x 1,000 shares = $500; $500 ÷ $9,000 = 5.5%) But what if XYZA's stock price went much higher? The potential for capital gains with the March

12.50 calls would be much greater—$3.50 per share ($12.50 – $9 = $3.50), or a total of $3,500. That sum, when combined with the option premium income of $500, would give you a total profit potential on the transaction of $4,000, or a possible total return of 44.4%.

So, now it is up to you to decide which option contract to write. There really is no right or wrong answer, only what you feel is right for you. Are you willing to take a reasonable return of 11.1% with an opportunity to make 22.2%, or do you wish to take only a 5.5% return for the chance to make a whopping 44.4%? The choice is yours. The good news is, no matter which choice you make, you are certain of an immediate return of at least 5.5% on your investment. However, you must examine all of your possibilities before making a final decision.

I always run the numbers (as we did above) before I make a decision on which option to write. I even run the numbers before I buy the stock itself. I look to see which stock gives me the highest yield and the best opportunity for profit. You should, too. By examining your choices in this way you will always come up with the investment solution that's right for you.

# Covered Call Guidelines

There are a few guidelines I believe you should consider when you are examining potential stocks to purchase for covered call writing.

➢ The stock should be of good quality and commensurate with your risk tolerance and investment objectives.

➢ There should have been some price movement (volatility) in the stock, and it should not have languished at a particular price level for a long period of time. If there has been little movement in a stock's price, there will be less interest in options on that stock, and therefore a much smaller market (i.e., fewer people who want to buy or sell options).

➢ I used to say that for covered calls, the underlying stock's price should be between $8 and $25 per share, but in view of the recent strength of the overall market, I've revised my guidelines. Now I believe that the underlying stock price can be between $10 and $40. Stocks at these prices allow for better diversification of your portfolio. Since you can only lose what you invest, lower priced stocks in a well-diversified portfolio also tend to reduce your exposure to large losses. Additionally, you have more profit opportunities and investment choices with lower priced stocks, because the option strike prices are in increments of only $2.50.

These are only a sampling of ideas to follow. I'm sure that you will establish additional rules for yourself as you continue to employ this strategy successfully over time.

# 17

# LEAPS

A nother category of option is *L*ong-term *E*quity *A*ppreciation *S*ecurities, or LEAPS. LEAPS are long-term options typically extending one or two years, with two years being the maximum time frame. LEAPS can be either calls or puts, and all LEAPS expire in January. In 2001, for example, you could buy a LEAP that expired in 2002, or one that expired in 2003. (Once a LEAP's expiration date is under a year, it converts into a January option.) Currently, there are about 400 companies on which you can trade LEAPS, and LEAPS are listed on all the options exchanges.

There are two advantages and two disadvantages to LEAPS. The advantages are, first, they have a longer timeline (a year or more before they expire, as opposed to weeks or months). Second, they are a cost-effective way to control expensive stocks for a long period of time.

For example, in 2000 Yahoo was trading at around $150 a share, but you could have purchased the 2002 LEAP at a strike price of 180 for around $33. Quite a difference in price! When I invest in LEAPS, I look for expensive stocks with a lot of volatility. By buying the LEAPS, I can benefit from the volatility and the price swings without investing a whole lot of money.

LEAPS also will give you a lot more time value for very little additional money. Let's say a six-month option in a volatile stock might be trading for $18. You might be able to buy the LEAP, which would give you 14 or 15 months' more time value, for around $21 or $22. So it would pay you to buy the LEAP rather than the six-month option.

Unfortunately, LEAPS are not heavily traded. That means the spread (the difference between the bid and the ask) is generally a lot wider than with other options. There can be upwards of a $2 or $3 difference, which means the LEAP has to rise in value a lot more for you to make the same kind of profit percentage as you would with shorter-term options. The second disadvantage is that LEAPS can be expensive when compared to other options, because you are getting so much more time value.

It will take a greater amount of your investment capital to get into them. But compared to the amount you would have to invest to buy some of the underlying stock (with prices of $150 and up), investing in LEAPS lets you take advantage of their volatility without an enormous capital outlay. So I use LEAPS as part of my overall portfolio.

## LEAPS and Covered Calls

Here's another reason I like LEAPS: you can use LEAPS as the basis for covered call writing. "What?" I can hear you say. "Write an option on an option? Are you crazy?" No—it's perfectly legal, and very smart. Like a covered call, where you write a call option on stock that's in your portfolio, *you can write a call option on LEAPS that you own, too.* (Obviously, you'd be writing a regular, short-term call that would expire in a few weeks.)

Why use LEAPS rather than stock for covered call writing? Remember, you can buy a LEAP on a stock that's trading for $150 a share for only $20 to $25. Why lay out $150 a share to buy stock on which you want to write covered calls, when you only need lay out $20 to $25 for the LEAP to do the same thing?

Here's the only thing you need to watch out for. What happens if you get "called away"—that is, someone decides to exercise the call you've sold on the LEAP? First of all, you try not to let that happen. You can always buy back the option you wrote, even if you have to buy it back at a loss. (I usually buy the option on expiration day, so I will get it at the cheapest possible price.) But remember, someone would exercise the call option only if the strike price of the LEAP was in the money—that is, the LEAP is now worth *more* than the strike price of the call. If you sold a call with a strike price of $20, and the LEAP is now at $25, the strike price is in the money by $5. So your underlying LEAP has increased in value more than the call option you've written on it. If you choose, on expiration day, you can just close out the whole position by selling your LEAP and buying back the call option. And since the LEAP has appreciated more than the option, you'll make money on the trade.

# 18

# Index Options

Index options are interesting investment vehicles for the more experienced investor who wishes to hedge an existing portfolio of stocks or take a speculative position in trading the stock market. Let's first learn what an index option is, then look at an example of how they are used, and finally, discuss how you can apply them profitably to your own investment strategies.

## The Index

An index is a way of measuring or evaluating a group of stocks based on their aggregate price. The index is a hypothetical value of the total stock prices, which are initially assigned an arbitrary representative value. (It's like asking someone how they feel on a scale of one to ten. They do not really "feel" like a number, but it is representative of how they feel, based on ten being great.) If we were to start our own stock index today using a portfolio of ten different stocks, we might assign the index an initial value of 100 based on the closing prices of those ten stocks. As those prices go up and down, the index will be increased or decreased correspondingly. Some stocks in the index may have greater weight than others because the increase or decrease in their price may have more of a dramatic effect on the overall change in stock market direction. Basically, that's what an index is in a nutshell.

There are three primary stock indexes traded on U.S. financial exchanges, and each represents a different value index. They are:

1) the Standard and Poor's 500 Index (SPX), which represents 500 stocks

2) the Standard and Poor's 100 Index (OEX), representing 100 stocks

3) the Major Market Index (XMI), which includes 20 stocks

The SPX (usually referred to as the S&P 500) includes 500 stocks which trade on both the New York Stock Exchange (NYSE) and on Nasdaq. It's like the "Fortune 500" list of companies, and is the broadest representation of overall stock market performance (perhaps the most popular of the indexes to watch). The S&P 100 (usually called the OEX) represents 100 stocks, nearly all of which trade on the NYSE, and includes the 30 stocks which make up the Dow Jones Industrial Average (DJIA). The Major Market Index, or the XMI, represents the 20 highest capitalized and widely recognized stocks listed on the NYSE. It currently comprises 19 of the 30 stocks in the DJIA; stocks such as IBM, Merck, GE, Procter & Gamble, Coca-Cola, AT&T and others, are also included.

**You can trade options—both puts and calls—on each of these indexes just as you can with stocks.** The index options have different strike prices, and they trade based on changes in the index value, just as stock options trade on the price changes of their respective stocks. Index option strike prices are usually set at five-point increments of the index value, and generally extend very deep in the money, as well as far out of the money.

To use an example of options strike prices, let's look at where the OEX index stands as of March

2001. The price of the OEX index is currently at 650.16. (It is sometimes helpful to look at an index's value like dollars and cents. There is a direct relationship in stock indexes, as you will see later.) There are options trading on this index with strike prices of 635, 640, 645, 650, 655, 660, 665, etc. As you can see, the strike prices are in increments of $5. New strike prices are added as needed (as demand indicates), i.e., whenever the index touches an existing strike price at the upper or lower end of the scale.

Remember, with each option contract represents 100 shares, so each one-point move in an option's price represents $100. In the same way, each one-point move in an index option represents $100, and the settlement of purchases and sales will occur the next business day. Trading in index options begins at 9:30 AM Eastern Time and extends until 4:15 PM. The options expire at the same time equity options do, so the last opportunity to trade them is the third Friday of the expiration month.

When getting a market quote on an index option, you would select the trading month (current month or following month) and the option strike price; then ask the broker for the quote. For example: "Please give me a quote on the OEX March 650 call options." The broker will respond with a market quote just as he would if he were quoting stock options: "The OEX March 650's are currently quoted at $8.90 by $9.40," for example. (Index options are already quoted in dollars and cents instead of fractions.) Index options trading is fairly easy and any broker should be able to assist you in placing your order.

## Uses of Index Options

Index options are used in two primary ways: for outright speculation, and for hedging an existing portfolio. As you might imagine, it's the speculation that fortunes are to be made quickly that entices everyone to trade the indexes. The value of the indexes changes dramatically during the average trading day; it is not unusual for the value of an index option to double at some point from its daily low. For the amateur, it is fairly unpredictable, though, and is little more than outright gambling on the direction of the market. More poor people than rich ones have been made from such activities in the past.

Should you decide to speculate in index options, there are many choices (strike prices) available. For example, the OEX index mentioned earlier was at 650.16 in March 2001, and there were options available at various strike prices. Each strike price has a different market price according to demand and proximity (in or out of the money) to the current value of the actual index. So, with the index at 650.16, you might receive the following quotes from your broker.

| | Bid | | Ask |
|---|---|---|---|
| **OEX Mar 640 calls** | 14.70 | x | 15.70 |
| **OEX Mar 640 puts** | 7.30 | x | 7.50 |
| **OEX Mar 645 calls** | 11.50 | x | 12.50 |
| **OEX Mar 645 puts** | 8.80 | x | 9.30 |
| **OEX Mar 650 calls** | 8.90 | x | 9.40 |
| **OEX Mar 650 puts** | 10.10 | x | 10.60 |
| **OEX Mar 655 calls** | 7.10 | x | 7.60 |
| **OEX Mar 655 puts** | 11.00 | x | 11.90 |
| **OEX Mar 660 calls** | 5.10 | x | 5.60 |
| **OEX Mar 660 puts** | 15.70 | x | 16.60 |

After getting these quotes, you would need to decide which option represented your best short-term opportunity for profit. But since many of these options would cost well over $1,000 or more (remember, you have to multiply the numbers on the ask side by 100 to determine how much you will pay per contract), you cannot afford to be wrong for long. Although it is probable that index options will change price rapidly throughout the day, it's a large investment to make in one option contract. Purchasing several contracts could be devastating should the market react opposite to your assumptions. However, the purchase of several contracts could also make you tens of thousands of dollars if the market reacts as you anticipated. (We will cover more about choosing option contracts a little later in this chapter.)

# Hedging Your Portfolio

Efficient use of index options can be a useful tool for hedging the potential decline of a stock portfolio. As I mentioned earlier, there are both call and put options available on the indexes, and puts give us a high degree of leverage and portfolio protection in declining markets. Puts, as you know, become more valuable as the index declines, and since the index represents the overall price movement of the stock market, it will obviously decline in value along with stock prices overall. By purchasing puts on one of the indexes you can effectively hedge much of the price decline in your stock portfolio.

I usually trade OEX options because they have great liquidity; many institutions trade these options, too. You may have an index that is a particular favorite, as I do. The important thing to remember is to **choose an index that best represents the make-up of your stock portfolio.** Selection of a broad-based index or one more narrow in scope should be commensurate with your overall investment objectives and the type of stocks you own.

I mentioned earlier that there was a relationship between the value of an index and its measurement in terms of dollars and cents. Let's examine that relationship so that we can determine the number of contracts necessary to effectively hedge our portfolio. Take, for example, the OEX index that was listed at a value of 650.16. This value actually represents a selected stock portfolio worth $65,016. Theoretically, then, this $65,016 portfolio could be hedged through the purchase of one (1) put option contract, since each contract would represent an index having the same dollar value. As the value of that $65,016 portfolio declines, the put options would increase in value (again, theoretically) by the same amount that the portfolio declined. Therefore, according to this theory, if you had a large portfolio worth $650,160, you would need to purchase ten (10) options contracts to effectively hedge it.

I use the term "theoretically" because in actual practice the forces of the market play a very large role in the price movements of index options. In practice, absolute stock price declines tend to be greater than the actual increases in the price of the put options. (Call options on the index, though, tend to increase in price more rapidly in upward markets than put options do in downward markets.) **In most market declines, the increase in option premiums of "at the money" put options are equal to roughly 60% of the actual decline in the price of the stocks.** What that means is, if you have a $65,016 portfolio, you would need to purchase two (2) "at the money" put option contracts (at a cost of $2,120) just to hedge against the decline in this manner. As the protection would last only until the options expired, I don't believe this is a reasonable sum of money to spend each month for portfolio protection.

How then, might we accomplish portfolio protection without spending such an unreasonable amount of money? I have found the best way to reasonably hedge against a portfolio decline without paying excessive portfolio "insurance" premiums is to **buy a current-month put option five (5) strike prices out of the money.** The purchase price of that option is nearly always less than one-half of what an "at the money" put option would cost, and it usually moves the equivalent of 55% as much as the "at the money" put option would. Therefore, if you were so inclined, you could actually buy *twice* as many "out of the money" put options for less than the price of the "at the money" options and still get more than 110% of the protection. However, no matter which index option you purchase, it's possible to hedge only about 60% of our portfolio decline, dollar for dollar, and be cost effective. So the purchase of one option, five strike prices out of the money, makes the most sense in the majority of cases.

Remember that hedging is really insuring against a potential loss, and most of us are willing to spend just so much money to hedge against a loss. You may wish to liken the payment of option premiums to an insurance premium. Your option "policy" covers only 55 to 60% of your costs; the rest of your portfolio either is uninsured or is the "deductible" portion of a loss that the policy does not cover. Unfortunately, the cost of complete and total coverage is greater than the potential loss in many cases, but nonetheless index option puts can be used as a reasonable hedge against a major decline in your portfolio's worth.

# Speculating With Index Options

Let's revisit, for now, how we might go about choosing the purchase of an index option contract to maximize our investment returns if we are speculating on price movements in the stock market. In the OEX index list on page 174, take a look at the call option prices for a moment. Let's assume that we have a strong feeling, based on our research, that the stock market is going to rise 10% over the next 30 days. The OEX index currently stands at the 650.16 level and, as we have indicated before, a 10% increase in the overall market would probably increase the index by about 10%, as well. That move, then, could propel the level of the OEX to nearly 715.00 (up 10%). With that index value increase, the index call options would have moved significantly higher as well. Let's see how much we might have made if we had invested in the call options and which call option series might have been the best one to buy. (Prices are before and after the stock market rise.)

| | Before (OEX at 650) | | | After (OEX at 715) | | |
|---|---|---|---|---|---|---|
| **OEX Mar 640 call** | 14.70 | x | 15.70 | 55.30 | x | 59.30 |
| **OEX Mar 645 call** | 11.50 | x | 12.50 | 52.60 | x | 54.60 |
| **OEX Mar 650 call** | 8.90 | x | 9.40 | 49.10 | x | 51.10 |
| **OEX Mar 655 call** | 7.10 | x | 7.60 | 47.20 | x | 48.20 |
| **OEX Mar 660 call** | 5.10 | x | 5.60 | 44.90 | x | 45.90 |

If we had purchased the March 650 call, which would have been an "at the money" option at the time of our proposed purchase, we would have paid approximately $940 per contract when buying on the offer (ask) side of the market. That option would have then risen to approximately $4,910 per contract in the ensuing market rise, and we would be able to sell it for that price when selling on the *bid* side of the market. The increase, then, in our investment would be a total of approximately $4,910 minus $940, or $3,970 (excluding commission). Our investment return would then be a robust 422%. Not bad for a few days' work. However, if we had purchased an "out of the money" option—say, the 655 call—our investment return would have been significantly better.

The OEX March 655 call would cost us $760 (7.60 on the ask side of the market). We could sell that call now at the bid price of $4,720, or a profit of $3,960. That would provide an investment return in excess of 521% ($3,960 divided by $760)—significantly better than what we would have gotten if we had purchased an "at the money" call option for a great deal more money.

Remember, when purchasing options, you can lose the entire amount of money that you invest, so it is better to invest a little, rather than a lot. Also, out of the money options will nearly always provide a better percentage investment return than at the money or in the money options. The same holds true for equity options, as well.

When speculating in index options, I usually buy an option four or five strike prices out of the money to maximize my returns and reduce my investment risk. That's the name of the game in options. If you desire to speculate in index options, the use of this strategy can be both fun and profitable when the market moves your way.

# 18

# Advanced Plays I: Straddles and Strangles

One of the best strategies to make money involves the simultaneous purchase of a call and a put on the same stock at the same strike price. This is called a *straddle*. The assumption is that no matter which way the stock moves, we will participate in that movement in a profitable manner. If the stock shows strong growth (upside movement) we would participate on the call side of the straddle. Conversely, should the stock show weakness, we would own a put that would increase in value as the stock declined.

At first glance, it may seem that this strategy is foolproof; but in the stock market, nothing is quite that simple. There are some necessary guidelines that must be followed so the transaction has a chance of being profitable and we don't get into a stock that has little if any chance of making us any money. Let's look at some of the criteria for stock selection, and then we'll review what techniques work best using this strategy.

## 1. Volatility

First and foremost, it is important that the stock has sufficient volatility. Yes, by using this strategy you can profit in either direction the stock moves, but the stock *must* move. If it stays at the same price it was when the transaction was initiated, you will nearly always lose on the trade. Therefore, you want volatility (up and down movement) in the stock.

Determining volatility is easy if you have the right tools. I use a charting service that provides daily price movement of the stock. (See Chapter 10 for more about charts.) I look for stocks that have chart patterns that tell me how much a stock has moved, in terms of price, over a fairly short period of time (volatility). Many stocks exhibit patterns with significant enough volatility to be profitable using this strategy. All you have to do is look through a series of charts to find the right stock.

Once you find a stock that looks like it could be a good trade, that stock can be kept in your arsenal to be played over and over again until it no longer meets the volatility criteria. Many times the same stock can be played for many months before it loses its volatility. Keep an eye on the chart as you trade, though, for signs of reduced trading activity and volatility. You will know as time goes on if this stock is one that you will want to continually play simply by watching its activity while you are still trading it.

The following chart pattern demonstrates the kind of volatility I look for in a straddle play.

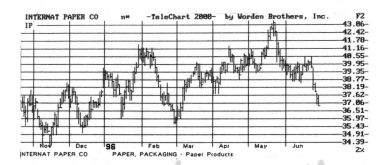

## 2. Price for the Combined Options

Knowing that volatility is the first thing you need, what comes next? You must determine the price you will pay for the combined options. If you were to watch a particular stock and found that it had jumped up dramatically due to a recent news item (earnings outlook, perhaps), you couldn't be sure if it would continue to go up or drop back to prior trading levels. But you believe it's either going to go up or down. At this point then, you decide to do your straddle. You would buy *both a put and a call at the same strike price with the same expiration date.* The key is to spend no more than a percentage of what you think the expected price movement in the stock will be. If you think that the stock could move up five points or go down five points, that's a ten-point swing. But if you pay too much for the combined options, you may never be able to profit even if the stock does what you want (and expect) it to do.

The rule of thumb in a straddle is, **never spend more than 50% of the expected movement of the stock for the call and put options combined.** If you think the stock could go up or down ten points, for example, you don't want to spend more than $5 for both the put and the call. Now, you might think, "That's a lot of money for options," but remember, you already determined this stock is volatile and would move in one direction or the other, and it would definitely *not* stay at its current price level. So you are fairly certain to make money on one side of the trade or the other.

Let's take a more specific example. If XYZ stock were at $75 per share, and you believe the stock will go up or down by at least ten points, you would buy the XYZ $75 puts and the XYZ $75 calls for a combined premium (option cost) of no more than $5 (50% of the expected movement of the price of the stock). If XYZ continues to move *up*, the *calls* will be worth more than the amount of money we would lose on the puts. If the stock goes *down* dramatically, the *puts* will be worth more than the amount lost on the calls.

Let's say that XYZ moved from $75 per share to $80 a few days after you bought the straddle. The $75 calls would be worth probably $6 to $7, and the $75 puts would be worth perhaps $1, for a combined value of $7 to $8. But remember, you purchased the calls and puts for a combined premium of $5. You've made about 40% to 60% on your investment. If you adhere to the rules of not paying more than 50% of the expected movement for the combined options, you should have many, many happy and profitable trading days.

# Strangles

There's a way to play this same strategy, though, with another technique that I like better because it requires less capital to execute. This technique is called a *strangle*. A strangle involves "surrounding" the stock with a purchase of both a put and a call, but at *different* strike prices. If XYZ stock was at $73 per share, for example, a strangle would involve the purchase of an XYZ $75 call and an XYZ $70 put. This surrounds the stock's current price and again allows for a profitable trade if the stock moves dramatically in either direction.

The rule of thumb for a strangle is **to not spend more than *30%* of the expected price movement for the purchase of both the put and call.** Because you are required to put up less money per transaction, you can purchase more contracts (and use more leverage) than with a conventional straddle. You *must* be sure that the stock will move, however. If the stock stays at the current level, you will lose on both sides of the transaction. Although the strangle offers greater leverage, it also has greater risk if the stock stagnates at its current price.

# 20

# Advanced Plays II: Option Spreads

L et's take a look at how another option strategy can be used profitably with a technique involving option spreads. A *spread* involves the purchase and sale of calls or puts on the same underlying stock at two different strike prices. In other words, if you *purchase* a call at one strike price, at the same time you would *sell* a call at a different strike price. If you purchased a put, you would sell a put at a different strike price. The investor hopes the underlying stock will move in the preferred direction (up for calls, down for puts) so that he or she may close out the transaction profitably with limited risk.

# Call Spreads

A *call* spread involves the purchase of a call option with a strike price typically lower than the strike price of the call that is sold. For example, say you wanted to execute an option spread on Microsoft (MSFT) stock. The stock is currently trading at around $61. You buy ten (10) MSFT June 60 calls at 2 3/4, for a total investment of $2,750 (10 contracts = 1,000 shares; 1,000 x $2 3/4 = $2,750). At the same time you write (sell) 10 MSFT June 65 calls at 7/8. Since you were the seller, you receive $875 in your portfolio account (1,000 x $7/8 = $875). The strike price of the option you *bought* (the MSFT June 60 calls) is lower than the strike price of the option you *sold* (the MSFT June 65 calls). You are limiting your risk by taking in a small profit now, thereby reducing the *net cost* of your transactions. You can figure out your net cost by subtracting the amount you took in when you sold the June 65 calls from the amount you paid to buy the June 60 calls.

| Buy 10 MSFT June 60 Calls @ 2 3/4 = | $2,750 |
| Sell 10 MSFT June 65 Calls @ 7/8 = | – $875 |
| Net Cost | $1,875 |

Even though you don't actually own the MSFT stock to cover the June 65 calls that you sold, this is still considered a "covered" transaction. Why? Because you bought the June 60 calls, and therefore you have the right to buy the stock at a lower price ($60) should you be exercised on the $65 call.

"Okay, Chuck," you say. "I see so far I've spent some money and made some money. The two transactions have still cost me $1,875. Where's the profit?" Simple: **if MSFT stays above the $60 strike price by an amount *greater* than the net cost of the transaction, you will make money.** In the above example, if MSFT moves above $61.875 ($60 + $1.875 per share), the transaction is profitable. Once that happens, you would close out the position by selling the $60 call and buying back the $65 call as one transaction. This is called "closing the spread."

If MSFT should move above $65, the maximum amount you can make is the difference between the two strike prices of the options. Therefore, if MSFT moved above $65 by June, you would close out the transaction and theoretically receive $5,000—the difference between the two strike prices of $60 and $65. (I use the word "theoretically" because the differential is closer to 4 3/4, with the remainder being the spread that the market maker takes relative to closing out the transaction.) Your *profit* would be the difference between $5,000 and the amount that you paid for the options ($1,875), or $3,125. You've "limited" your profit potential to 166% (not bad).

An option spread can be developed at different time intervals, or it can be accomplished simultaneously, with the purchase and sale of the options occurring at once. When executed simultaneously, you would give your broker an order using the term *net debit*. This means that the purchase and sale of the options contracts will result in a net cost not to exceed the net debit amount. Using the above example, you would figure out your costs for buying the June $60 calls and selling the June $65 calls, and then place the order using a net debit of 1 7/8. The price of both option contracts may continue to change rapidly in a fast-moving market but the stockbroker will not execute your trades unless you pay the equivalent of $1 7/8 or less.

A spread may be developed individually as well. You start by purchasing a particular option contract as an initial or "opening" transaction. As the underlying stock begins to move in the desired direction, you can limit your risk by writing another option contract, thereby bringing money into your account and reducing the cost basis of the investment in the original contract purchased.

Say you purchased those ten MSFT June 60 calls at 2 3/4. You spent $2,750 immediately; but you'd like to limit your risk (remember, options can expire, leaving you with nothing) and you're willing to take a little less profit in the end to do so. You call your broker and instruct him or her to sell ten contracts of MSFT June 65 calls. The option sells at $7/8, netting you $875. Your cost basis (the amount you have invested in the two transactions) is now $1,875 instead of $2,750. MSFT stock now has to rise only $1.875 per share instead of $2.75 for you to recoup the cost of your investment. If it does *better* than that, you stand to gain greater profits. If the stock price doesn't move the way you thought it would, your downside potential is $1,875 instead of $2,750. (You probably wouldn't lose the whole amount anyway, because you would get out if the value of those June 60 calls dropped below 50% of what you paid for them—see Chapter 11, "Stock Terms.")

There's another type of call spread that works very well in a declining (bear) market—a *credit call spread*. This is a little more tricky, because you are going to be writing "naked" call options (meaning, you own neither the underlying stock nor an option that will allow you to purchase the stock at a lower strike price). Here's how a credit call spread works. Say company "ABCD" is currently trading at $30 a share. The overall market has been declining steadily, and you think that ABCD is also going to either stay at $30 or move down with the market. The September 30 calls are selling for $1 1/2, so you write ten (10) contracts of the September 30s, bringing in $1,500. At the same time, you buy ten contracts of the September 35s, which are going for $ 3/8. You spend $375, so your net profit is $1,125. You're protected in case the stock goes way up, because you have the right to buy the stock at $35 a share, which will cover the $30 call you wrote (sold) without owning the underlying stock. You'll lose the $5 a share difference, but that loss will be offset by the $1,125 profit you took in. And since the market and ABCD have been trending lower, it's not likely that kind of rise in the stock price will occur. If ABCD's stock price stays where it is or drops below $30, no one will want to exercise the $30 call you sold, you certainly won't exercise the $35 call option you bought! Both options will expire unexercised, and you will keep the $1,125.

Spreads can be used for several reasons, particularly when you want to reduce the cost of an option transaction and you're also willing to limit your profit potential (again, to a maximum of the difference between the two strike prices).

# Put Spreads

Typically call spreads are the most popular, but put spreads can work well in a bear market. In a put spread, the investor will purchase an option having a higher strike price than a put that he sells. (This also is considered a covered transaction.) As the stock declines, the puts become more valuable. When the stock declines to a point where both options are in the money or the far option contract is at the money (i.e., the strike price and the current stock selling price are the same), the investor will liquidate the position, which has reached its maximum potential profit level. This transaction, too, can be executed individually or as a unit.

Let's take the same example of MSFT. This time, you think MSFT's stock is going to go down. It's currently trading at $61 a share. You sell ten MSFT June 55 puts at $3/4, taking in $750. At the same time you purchase ten MSFT June 60 puts at $2 1/2, for a total cost of $2,500. Your net cost for the two transactions is $1,750 ($2,500 – $750 = $1,750).

As the days go by, MSFT does what you expect: it drops. As the stock price declines, your puts become more valuable, both the one you bought and the one your sold. Once MSFT drops below $60, to $58, for example, the June 60 puts which you bought are now in the money—meaning, the strike price is above the price where the stock is currently selling.

Whenever an option is in the money, its price is going to rise by *at least* the amount of the difference between the strike price and the current stock price—in this case, $2 ($60, the strike price, minus $58, the price at which the stock is currently selling).

But wait—what about the June 55 puts you *sold?* Those, too, have gone up in value, as MSFT's current stock price has gotten closer to the $55 level. But it hasn't gone up as much as the June 60 puts, because it isn't in the money yet—its strike price is still below the stock's current selling price.

This trade will reach its maximum profit potential as soon as (or if) MSFT drops to $55 or below. At that point, the June 60 puts you bought are worth at least $5 each—the difference between the strike price of the put ($60) and the current price of the stock ($55). The put you *sold,* however, is at the money, meaning that the strike price and the stock's current selling price are the same ($55). So you would sell the ten June 60 puts for at least $5 each—probably more like $6 or $7. At the same time you would need to buy back the ten June 55 puts you sold (so you could cover your obligation). However, since the June 55 puts are at the money, you will probably spend around $1 each.

Here's what your net profit would look like:

**Transaction 1:**

| | |
|---|---:|
| Buy 10 MSFT June 60 Puts @ 2 1/2 = | $2,500 |
| Sell 10 MSFT June 55 Puts @ 3/4 = | − $750 |
| Net Cost | $1,750 |

**Transaction 2:**

| | |
|---|---:|
| Sell 10 MSFT June 60 Puts @ 6 = | $6,000 |
| Buy 10 MSFT June 55 Puts @ 1 = | −$1,000 |
| Profit | $5,000 |

**Net Profit from Spread:**

| | |
|---|---:|
| Profit from Transaction 2 | $5,000 |
| Cost from Transaction 1: | −$1,750 |
| Net Profit | $3,250 |

Generally speaking, spreads liquidated as a unit will usually result in better execution prices for the investor. I recommend that spreads be liquidated together to maximize price and yield potential. When liquidating, the order given to the broker would be for a *net credit* (rather than a net debit) amount, and would be executed if the price reaches that net credit level or higher.

# Using Spreads Like Covered Calls

Spreads can also be used in the same manner as covered calls. We think of writing covered calls for income purposes and for portfolio hedges, but spreads can also be used to generate income on higher priced stocks rather than buying the stock itself. Why use spreads? Even if you were to purchase a high-priced stock on margin, it would probably require more investment capital than a well-planned spread.

Let's look at the following example to illustrate this point. If you were to purchase 1,000 shares of IBM stock with the stock being around $130 per share, you would need at least $65,000 in cash to execute the trade, even on a 100% margin basis. Since your goal is to make money if IBM stock increases, you may be able to accomplish the same task by purchasing ten contracts of the IBM $115 calls (which would be deep in the money) for about $20, and writing (selling) the IBM $140 calls for about $6. The net cost would then be approximately $14,000 (the $20,000 you paid for ten contracts of the IBM $115 calls at $20 per share, minus the $6,000 you made by selling ten contracts of the IBM $140 calls at $6 per share) rather than $65,000.

If IBM stock were to climb to $140 per share or higher, the spread can then be liquidated at a net credit of $25,000. Here's how. When IBM's stock price hits $140 a share, the calls you bought at a strike price of $115 are $25 in the money, and are now worth *at least* $25 each ($140 − $115 = $25) because of intrinsic value. So you would direct your broker to sell your ten $115 calls, and buy ten $140 calls (once again, covering your position) for a net credit of $25,000. (Remember, these two transactions would be executed as a unit for a net credit.)

This trade, then, would result in a net profit of $11,000 (your net credit of $25,000 minus your net cost of $14,000), or a cash-on-cash return of approximately 78%. This strategy also requires much less investment capital than the outright purchase of the stock.

# Calendar Spreads

A calendar spread is one where the underlying purchased option contract has a maturity *longer* than that of the contract that is written or sold. It is not unusual for this strategy to be employed when option contracts are purchased on higher-priced stocks (as in the IBM example above). On many occasions an investor may purchase a long-term call, thinking the price may rise over time, yet write a short-term call thinking that the stock may stay in a lower range in the near term. Calendar spreads can also be used very effectively with LEAPS (see Chapter 17) as an income producer, as well as long-term equity appreciation investments.

# Rules of Thumb for Spreads

There are a few guidelines to remember when executing spread transactions that will help us maximize your profit potential and limit possible losses.

1. Limit any net debit amount to no more than 50% of the difference between strike prices. (For example, if the strike prices are five points

apart, we should not pay more than $2.50 as a
net debit, maximum.)

2. In most spread transactions, the most you can
   usually make is twice your investment. Don't
   get too greedy! If you get only a 50% or 75%
   return, be happy and get out.

3. Invest only in option contracts of volatile
   stocks.

4. Use limit orders when liquidating spread
   transactions.

5. Liquidate the spread as a unit, not separately,
   to get the best execution prices.

# Section IV

# Making Money in a Bear Market

Remember the old saying, "What goes up must come down"? Since 1992 and throughout the 1990s, the U.S. was in one of the longest bull markets ever. And because many people didn't begin investing until the 1990s, they'd never experienced a bear market—until 2001.

Everybody hates a bear market, right? We turn on the news, check with our broker, or check our Internet trading account, and all we see is stock value plummeting. There's a sense of unease, if not doom and gloom, in the air. All the value we've been building so carefully in our buy and hold portfolio is vanishing before our very eyes. This is the time we decide all this investing stuff just isn't for us, and we pull everything out of the market and put it into CDs, T-bonds, money markets—anything but stocks.

But bear markets (defined as drop of at least 20% from peak levels of the S&P 500 index) are an inevitable part of the economic cycle. If you are committed to being an investor for longer than ten years, you're undoubtedly going to encounter at least one bear market in your investing lifetime, so you'd better figure out how to make the most of it.

In truth, a bear market can provide some of the *greatest* opportunities for the savvy investor to make money. If you can manage your emotions, stay realistic while not buying in to the general feeling of pessimism that accompanies most bear markets, you can use this time to actually increase your wealth.

In this section we'll discuss how you can profit from a bear market by

➢ protecting the value of your portfolio by changing its composition,

➢ using strategies that allow you to make money when stocks go down, and

➤ protecting yourself whenever a financial transaction doesn't go the way you want it to.

In the poem, "If," by Rudyard Kipling, there's a line which says, "If you can keep your head while those around you are losing theirs...." In a bear market, it can seem like everyone around you is losing his or her head. But as long as you keep your eyes open and your head together, you'll find dozens of opportunities to make money in *any* market—bull, bear, or in between.

# Winning Wealth Strategies

# 21

# Your Bear Market Portfolio

In a bear market, the propensity is for market forces—which include everything from general market indicators like consumer spending, to companies missing their earnings forecasts, to the Fed chairman choosing to reduce interest rates or not, and so on—to go against you and have a negative effect on the value of your investments. So your first goal in a bear market should be to reduce your exposure to *all* market forces, be they good or bad. Usually that begins by looking at the composition of your current investment portfolio.

## "Lighten Up"

If your portfolio is mostly cash, then you're in great shape, ready to use the strategies in this section to capitalize on investment opportunities in the bear market. However, most people have at least some stocks in their portfolio. If this is true for you, then you need to take a look at your stocks with the idea of "lightening up." That means, first of all, *sell your losers*. As I said in Chapter 13, this is often the toughest thing for us to do psychologically. But especially in a bear market, you need to dump stocks that aren't performing for you.

Now, if these stocks are in the buy and hold section of your portfolio, you probably bought them because you believed in the company's ability to make money for you in the long term. A bear market is a time to *re-examine each of your buy and hold investments* to make sure the company's fundamentals are still strong. It's one thing to have a position in General Electric, for example, where the company's earnings, sales, corporate direction, and so on, are sound and strong enough to weather a bear market downturn. But if you put your money in something like Chrysler—where the company's fundamentals changed significantly when they were bought by Daimler-Benz—it might be time to put your money into something else. So for your buy and hold investments, check the fundamentals and confirm you want to continue to own this stock. If not, sell it, take your profits or losses, and put the money into something that will do better for you in the current economic climate.

## Diversify, Diversify, Diversify

In a bear market, if you are heavily invested in one particular stock or industry, you can get killed. And with the employee stock ownership plans many companies offer today, I see a lot of people whose entire portfolio consists of stock in the company they work for. That's not a smart strategy for any market climate, but in a bear market it can be catastrophic. I'm sure a lot of folks who work for Cisco or Microsoft or Qualcomm or Yahoo thought they had it made when they amassed tens of thousands of shares of their company's stock—and they've watched the value of their holdings shrink significantly in just a few months.

When your employer's losing money you have enough to worry about; the composition of your stock portfolio shouldn't add to your woes. So do yourself a favor: *diversify*. There are so many opportunities out there to make money during a bear market. There are some sectors (like the "sin" industries—tobacco and alcohol) that do extremely well when the rest of the economy is suffering. Take advantage of cheaper stock prices to spread your investment dollar across different sectors and industries, and create a more balanced portfolio that will hold its value in bull and bear markets alike.

# Upgrade to Higher-Quality Stocks

In your buy and hold portfolio, you can also *upgrade the quality of the stocks you own.* In bear markets, even high-quality stocks lose some of their value. (Some people would say stocks lose a lot of their *inflated* value during bear markets.) So you can purchase a lot more shares of stock in great companies at much lower prices.

You can either look for stock in great companies in any industry, or you can look to upgrade your holdings within a particular industry or sector. Say for some reason, you wanted exposure to the transportation sector and/or the airline industry, so you've bought a lot of

Southwest Airlines stock—a good company, but not a first-tier airline. During a bear market, you might want to sell your Southwest shares and buy United or AMR (parent of American Airlines), both large, established airlines. When the market moves into a more positive climate, United and AMR will probably move up faster than Southwest, thereby giving you greater profit potential with their stock.

If you want to *add* to your buy and hold stocks during a bear market, be patient. In a bear market, the price of even quality stocks isn't going to "run away" from you, jumping upwards by large amounts without warning. I recommend you pick the price at which you want to invest in this particular quality company, and wait for the stock price to drop to that point.

And while you're waiting, why not bring some additional revenue into your portfolio by writing a put option on the stock you want to own? Say you've been looking at "MNOP," a fictional quality company whose stock has been trading in the mid-50's. You'd like to own some MNOP but you don't want to pay any more than $50 a share for it. So you could write (sell) a put for MNOP with a strike price of $50. If the stock drops to $50 before the option expiration date, the put will be exercised and you'll have to buy the stock for $50 a share. But wait—isn't that what you *wanted* to pay for it? And in truth, you're paying less than $50 a share, because you brought in income from selling the put. And if MNOP doesn't drop to $50, you simply keep the profits from selling the put, and (if you choose) do the same thing next month! (We'll talk more about selling puts in Chapter 23, "Defensive Strategies.")

Remember, you want to reduce your exposure to market forces, so I recommend that you keep no more than about 50% of your portfolio in stocks during a bear market. You can make sure that 50% are high-quality stocks, but there are a lot of other places for you to put your money that will provide much greater returns in this particular economic climate.

## Convertible Bonds

If you want to keep part of your portfolio in stocks and we're in a bear market scenario where interest rates are coming down, one of my favorite investment vehicles is the *convertible bond.* Convertible bonds are sold by companies (unlike the T-bonds described in Chapter 7, which are sold by the U.S. government), and have different ratings (AAA, AA, B, etc.) to tell you how safe they are. Most convertible bonds are sold in units of $1,000 with a minimum purchase amount of $5,000, so you could buy a $5,000 bond, a $6,000 bond, and so on. Convertibles are fixed-rate bonds, which means they pay a certain percentage interest rate no matter what, and the interest is generally paid every six months. The bonds are usually for a term of ten years or longer.

Convertible bonds have all the advantages of most bond investments. They pay a fixed rate of interest at regular intervals. They're usually pretty highly rated, so for the most part they're a safe investment. Fixed-rate bonds always increase in price when interest rates go down, so the value of the bond itself will probably appreciate in a bear market with declining interest rates.

But the difference between convertible bonds and any other kind of bond is, *convertible bonds can be exchanged (converted) for a specific number of shares of stock in the company that issued the bond.* This conversion happens at the discretion of the bondholder, after a certain holding period.

Here's how it works. Let's say Ford Motor Company issues a ten-year convertible bond, maturing in June 2011. The interest rate on the bond is a little lower than you'd see on a regular bond, maybe 5% instead of 8%, so the company gets to borrow money at cheaper rates. But in exchange for accepting a little lower interest rate, the bondholder can convert each $1,000 bond to, say, 30 shares of Ford common stock any time after June 2004. (From now until June 2004 is the holding period.) You purchase $5,000 of Ford convertible bonds, and every six months you receive an interest payment of $125 (5% annually on your $5,000 investment).

Now, let's assume that we continue in a bear market, and interest rates keep declining. The value of your convertible bonds has increased, helping to offset any erosion in the value of your portfolio. But wait! As interest rates come down, is it possible that more people will be interested in buying cars? And the more people who buy cars, is it possible that Ford Motor Company's stock will rise in value, too? So not only is the value of the bond increasing, but the value of the shares the bond can be converted into is rising as well. (Remember, the bond is convertible for a certain number of shares, not a certain dollar value. Your $1,000 bond will get you 30 Ford shares, whether those shares are trading for $33 or $40 or $60.)

There are three different ways you can make money on a convertible bond. First, you can use it as a source of a set amount of income every six months. Second, you can treat it like a bond, allowing it to appreciate in value as interest rates decline and then selling it for a profit. Third, you can keep it until the holding period is up and exchange it for stock. Convertibles give you the safety and income potential of a bond combined with the ability convert your investment into the stocks when the holding period is up.

Of course, with convertible bonds as with any other investment vehicle, you need to make sure it makes sense for you. Ask yourself the following questions:

➤ *Do you want to own stock in this company and this industry?* If you don't like the company's prospects now, it's unlikely you'd want to own the stock a few years down the road. There are plenty of quality companies offering convertible bonds, so if you don't like Ford you can buy GM, or if you don't like Caterpillar you can buy Deere. Or if you don't like the auto industry, maybe there's a convertible bond you like in the transportation sector.

➤ *Is the interest rate high enough?* You want to make sure that you're bringing in a high enough rate of return to justify putting your investment dollars into this particular bond. Plus, if something should go wrong with the company and the value of the stock side of the convertible bond go way down, no one's going to want to buy the bond on the open market unless the interest rate is high enough. For example, AT&T used to have convertible bonds that would convert at a rate of about $40 per share. Well, when AT&T dropped to $20 a share its conversion feature was a lot less attractive. However, the bond paid interest at around 6.9%, a fairly high number, so there was still a market for the bond.

➤ *What's the conversion price?* I love it when the bond's conversion value is at parity with the stock—that is, the current value of the number of shares the bond can be converted into is equal to the face value of the bond. (In the Ford Motor Company example, where a $1,000 bond was convertible into 30 shares of stock, the bond would reach parity when the stock hit around $33 per share.) But I'll also look for convertible bonds where the conversion number is within 10 to 20% of the stock's current price. If the bond is convertible at a rate of $40 per share, and the stock's at $35, that's reasonable. If the stock's at $24, I'll look elsewhere, because I'm unlikely to be able to convert the bond to my advantage in a bear market (where stock prices are more likely to go down than up).

In a bear market, I'm very likely to have as much as 50% of my portfolio in convertible bonds. Why? Why *not*? Instead of being 50% invested in Chrysler stock, for example, why not sell the stock and invest in Ford convertible bonds? I earn interest on the bond, I can trade the bond if interest rates continue to decline, and if the value of the stock goes up, I can convert the bond into stock in what may be a more favorable economic climate a few years from now. And since convertible bonds are a cheaper way for large companies to raise capital, many of the largest and best companies around offer convertible bonds.

One final caveat about convertible bonds: only in situations where interest rates are coming *down* do you want to invest in bonds. When rates go down, bond prices go up, and the value of your investment increases. If inflation starts to rise, the Federal Reserve will keep interest rates higher, and then bonds won't be as attractive an investment. So as long as inflation is not a factor, bonds—and convertible bonds in particular—are a great investment alternative.

# 22

# Selling Short

As I said in Chapter 14, almost everyone understands the concept of "buy low, sell high." But you can make just as much money selling high and then buying back low. In fact, selling high and buying low is one of the few ways to make money in a bear market. How do you do that? It's called *selling short.* You borrow the stock from your brokerage, sell it, wait for the stock price to drop, then buy the stock back at the lower price.

Simple concept, right? So simple that there are thousands of investors doing it every single day, making good money in a market where other investors are losing their shirts. In fact, there is an entire segment of the investment community called "bear market investors," who look for industries and sectors that aren't doing well and then sell those stocks short. If you want to know how to profit from almost any kind of market—bull or bear, up or down—you need to master this concept of "sell high, buy low."

Let's start with the basics. What kind of stock do you want to choose for selling short? One whose price you think is going to drop, of course. How do you find these stocks? Look at the news, at events you believe might occur in the near future *and* might also have an adverse effect on a particular company, industry, or sector. For example, you hear there's going to be an OPEC meeting next week, and you read news reports that say OPEC ministers are probably going to raise the price of crude oil. Crude oil is currently at $20 a barrel, and the ministers are threatening to raise the benchmark price up to $28 or $30. If they do, fuel prices are likely to go up, right?

Now, which industries might be adversely affected by a rise in the price of oil? Transportation industries—airlines, trucking, package delivery services like UPS and FedEx, etc.—will be hurt because they can't raise prices enough to make up for the increase in fuel costs. When costs go up, profitability gets squeezed. If profitability goes down, what happens to the price of a stock? It usually goes down as well. So it seems that the transportation sector might present some excellent opportunities for selling short.

Once you decide to look at transportation companies, you then go to *Barron's*, *Investor's Business Daily*, the financial pages of your local newspaper, or the financial area of a Website like Yahoo, AOL, or Quicken. There you find a listing of 20 transportation stocks, all of which are candidates for your short play. But before you proceed, you need to check the chart patterns for these particular stocks. (Remember Chapter 10?) You're looking for bearish chart patterns, which indicate a fundamental weakness in the stock's performance. Patterns like a reverse bowl, head and shoulders, or a stock breaking below its 90-day line of support are all bearish patterns.

Let's say you look at XYZ, which is one of the largest U.S. trucking companies. XYZ has a head and shoulders pattern, with a high followed by a dip, then a higher high, then another dip, then finally a third high, making the right shoulder. (See the next page for a sample graph.)

## GRAPH FOR XYZ TRUCKING

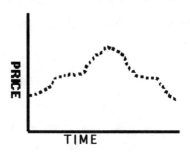

*(head and shoulders pattern)*

XYZ Trucking is in an industry that will likely be hit hard by any increase in oil prices, and its chart pattern is bearish. You check the newspaper and see it's been trading at around $30 a share. The OPEC meeting is coming up next week, and you decide you'd like to take advantage of this opportunity to profit from the potential downward movement in XYZ's stock price.

So you call your broker and say, "Tom, I don't like the chart pattern on XYZ Trucking. I also think the price of oil's going to go up, so I'd like to short the stock."

"Okay," he replies. "Let me check to see if we have any XYZ in inventory." (If your brokerage firm doesn't have any of the stock, don't worry; they can borrow it from another firm.) Tom checks his computer, then comes back on the line. "We have XYZ," he reports. "Currently the bid is $30.10. How much do you want to short?"

"I'd like to short 1,000 shares," you say. And later in the day, you check with Tom to find that you sold 1,000 shares of XYZ Trucking at $30. (You sold it at the market, so the price came in a little lower.) You now have $30,000 in your portfolio from selling XYZ short. Congratulations!

But you've only done one-half of the transaction, right? You've sold high, but you've also sold something you don't own—you've gone "short." (And going short isn't a bad thing. I've been short all my life!) Eventually you're going to have to buy 1,000 shares of XYZ to cover your short sale. You're betting that, with a rise in the price of oil after the OPEC meeting next week, you'll be able to buy XYZ at a price lower than you sold it for. But just to make sure you don't lose your shirt, what do you need to do? Use a stop order, as described in Chapter 11. Only in this case, you're going to use a *buy-stop* order. You're going to tell your broker that if XYZ goes above

$33 a share, he's to buy 1,000 shares at the market to cover your short sale. That way, your loss is limited to around 10%, and you're out of the position before you can get really hurt.

(The only way you can get badly hurt in a short sale is if the stock doesn't go down like you expected, but instead starts to run up. Without a buy-stop order, you'd have to buy back the stock at the market whenever you happened to notice it had started to rise. And if the stock is volatile, or the news you expected never materializes, you can lose your shirt very, very quickly.)

You've now sold short 1,000 shares of XYZ. You have $30,000 in your portfolio, and you have placed a buy-stop order at $33 to limit your downside potential. You have an obligation to purchase 1,000 shares of XYZ some time in the future to cover your short sale, but meanwhile you sit back and wait for the OPEC meeting.

The following week, the OPEC ministers do indeed decide to raise oil prices. The stock market anticipated the decision, however, so when you check the price of XYZ that week, it's dropped only by a point. Over the next couple of weeks, though, it continues trending downward—25 cents, one day, 50 cents the next, 75 cents the day after that. At the end of the month, XYZ is trading at $23 per share. *Time to take my profit,* you think, so you call Tom. "I want to close out my short position on XYZ," you say. "Buy me 1,000 shares at the market."

"I'll call you later with the price," he replies. Sure enough, at the end of the day he calls and reports, "You bought 1,000 shares of XYZ at 22.80." The shares of XYZ are automatically transferred back to the brokerage account they were borrowed from, and your short position is now closed.

What did you just do? You sold high, and bought low. You sold XYZ at $30 a share, and bought it at $22.80. You made a $7,200 profit on the short sell ($30 – $22.80 = $7.20 x 1,000 = $7,200), or a 31.5% profit (your profit, $7,200, divided by your outlay, $22,800, equals 31.5%). Pretty decent money on a stock whose price has dropped!

Do you see how simple selling short really is? Can you see how it's one of the best strategies for profiting in a bear market, where many of the stocks you've been following are probably going down in price? Far too many people say to me, "I just don't feel comfortable selling short and trying to make money while a stock is going down. I'd rather wait until it hits bottom, then I'll buy a lot of it and profit on the way back up." That strategy is called "bottom-fishing," and frankly, it doesn't make a lot of sense to me. Any stock you buy at the bottom might take a very long time to come back up. In general, it takes stocks a lot longer to rise than it does for them to fall. So why not make money on the way down instead?

There is a way to ease yourself into a short position that helps you cover your bases, in case the premise on which you're basing your decision to go short is wrong. This strategy is called *staging in,* and it's one I use a lot in bear markets. Let's go back to the XYZ example. Suppose the OPEC meeting is next month instead of next week. Oil prices have been rising slightly for a few months, but you believe once the OPEC meeting happens, they're going to go up a lot further a lot faster. Once that happens, XYZ Trucking should take a hit. You still want to short XYZ, but you're not as confident about the best timeline to get into the position. So instead of selling short 1,000 shares of XYZ now, you sell 300 at $30 each.

Two weeks from now, XYZ is going up a little (oil prices are holding steady), so you sell 300 more shares at $32. A week later, with the OPEC meeting less than a week away, rumors are flying that oil prices are going up, and XYZ drops back to $31. *Now's a good time to stage in the rest of the way,* you think, and you sell 400 shares of XYZ at $31. Once you've completely staged into your 1,000-share position, you put in a buy-stop at 10% above your average sale price, which in this case is $31. So your buy-stop is placed at $34.10.

Another week goes by, the OPEC meeting happens, and oil prices do indeed go up. Over the next several weeks XYZ's price drops, and you cover your short position at $23 a share. But you end up making more money because you sold short at $30, $32, and $31.

In some cases with staging in, you'll find things begin to move your way more quickly than you thought. If, for example, there was a major disruption in oil supplies a week after you sold short the first 300 shares of XYZ, the price might drop to $24 or $25 a share even without the OPEC meeting. If that happened, you might decide to take your profits and run, especially if you don't think XYZ will drop much further. If you think the price will come back up before it drops down again, you might let your 300 shares ride and see if you could sell some more XYZ short at a higher price point. But no matter what, staging in allows you to get some exposure to the benefits of selling short even if you're not certain of the timeline or effect of news.

## Using Options with Short Sales

You can actually increase your income on a short sale with the judicious use of puts. Let's continue to use our XYZ Trucking example. You sold XYZ short at $30 a share, and you know that eventually you're going to have to buy 1,000 shares of XYZ to cover your short position. What if you were to write a put on XYZ at a strike price of $25? Remember, a put gives someone the right to make you buy XYZ at $25 a share—but that would mean you'd cover your short and profit by at least $5 a share on the transaction, right? Plus, you'd have the income from writing the put in the first place. If by some chance XYZ didn't drop to $25 a share, the put would expire and you'd keep the profits from the option sale no matter what. Can you see how writing puts with your short sales can generate additional income?

You can also use puts that are further out of the money. In the above example, instead of writing a put with a $25 strike price, you could write one at $20 (which is a lot more out of the money). The $20 puts are not going to bring in as much income as the $25's—perhaps $400 for ten contracts (1,000 shares)—but as it's unlikely that XYZ is going to drop to $20 before the option expires, you probably won't be exercised. That $400 will then be pure profit. And if XYZ does drop below $20, you will have made $10 per share on the short position.

## Tips for Selling Short

There are three things to remember when utilizing the strategy of short selling. First, *selling short requires a margin account.* (Makes sense, since you're basically borrowing the stock in order to sell it, right?) Most brokerages have a margin equity requirement of somewhere between $3,000 and $5,000 cash in your account for you to sell short.

Second, *selling short is a momentum investment.* There's no official time limit for closing out a short position; you can be short a week, a month, a year, five years, whatever. But there are disadvantages to holding a short position too long. What if news comes in that causes the stock price to rise? What if the company becomes a mergers and acquisition target? You can really get hurt if someone comes in and says they're going to acquire XYZ Trucking and they're paying $73 a share, and you're short at $30. In many cases, if the market is going to move against you in a short position, it's going to move very hard and very fast, so I strongly recommend you set a time limit on your short positions. It's better to be satisfied with a smaller profit than be stuck holding a short position for a long time.

Third, *be careful of shorting stocks which pay dividends.* Say XYZ Trucking pays a quarterly dividend that's due the week after the OPEC meeting. The person who bought the 1,000 shares you sold short will receive the dividend from XYZ. But what about the brokerage firm you borrowed the shares from originally? Aren't they entitled to the dividend, too? And who's responsible for paying the dividend on those borrowed shares? You are—and your brokerage will automatically deduct it from your account. So you might want to either a) choose only non-dividend-paying stocks for your short positions, b) set your time limit to get out of the short position before the dividend is due, or c) pay the dividend and take the charge against your potential profits. I like to set my time limits, get out, and take a smaller profit if necessary.

When you sell short, you must keep a careful eye on the market movement of your particular positions. Many times, positive news concerning a stock that has been trending lower will create what's called a "short squeeze." This is when all the people who have sold the stock short try to cover their positions at the same time, so there are a lot of buyers but very few sellers. This drives the price of the stock upward very quickly, and the market makers in those stocks tend to widen the spreads on their quotes for the stock. They make a lot more money and you pay a higher price—but isn't that the way it always works in any supply and demand module? That's why buy-stop orders are so important on your short positions. But with some good preliminary research, a sense of how news can drive the market, and a willingness to take a smaller profit rather than holding out for what may be a fictional rate of return, you can make very good money in a bear market by selling short.

# 23

# Defensive Strategies

Every investment has the potential to do
well—or go wrong. If it does well, you've got
to know when to get out of it to maximize your
profits while minimizing your risk. If it goes wrong,
you darn well better know when and how to get
out of it so you don't lose your shirt. You must
know your exit strategy going in, and you must
have a defensive strategy ready in case your
investment starts to sour.

Remember, every investment has the potential
to be a total loss. Companies go bankrupt. Stock
becomes worthless. Options expire. Commodities
lose their value. Currencies undergo devaluation.
Luckily, all of this rarely happens at the same time
to the same investor! But my point is, every
investment has a potential down side, and if
you're smart, you'll protect yourself up front.

I've discussed several exit and defense strategies throughout this book, and I'll add more here. But the primary defense strategy for any investment is simply to *do the opposite*. If you bought a stock, option, or bond that's not doing what you want it to, sell it. If you sold something, buy it back. You may lose money on the deal, but it'll probably be a lot less than if you just let the investment ride. Cut your losses and move on. There's bound to be somewhere else you can put your money that *will* produce a profit, no matter what the current economic condition. After all, more people became millionaires during the Great Depression of the 1930s than in any time prior in U.S. history. There's always money to be made, so don't leave yours languishing in an investment that just isn't panning out.

## Exit Strategies: When to Sell

Here are a few basic rules that will help you decide when it's time to sell.

➢ **If the situation on which you based your investment decision changes.** Remember the OPEC oil ministers meeting in the last chapter?

What if they decided *not* to raise oil prices? Then the original premise on which you sold short was wrong, and you'd better get out of the position quickly. With a long-term buy and hold investment, if the fundamentals of the company change (different management team, no longer a market leader, decreased sales or earnings, etc.) it may be a sign to put your money elsewhere.

With options, if you were betting that the stock or the market was going in one direction and it starts heading in another, don't hesitate—get out. Options are time-sensitive (expiring after what is often a relatively short time), and hesitation can cost you your entire investment. Get out, take your losses, and find another investment opportunity.

➢ **If you have reached your profit target.** Whenever you invest, you should have a number in mind that represents the profits you want to make on this particular opportunity. However, there's a real temptation to "let it ride" when things are going your way. *Don't.* Whenever you reach your profit target, take a careful look at the investment to evaluate how much more room there is for it to rise. You may have already benefited from 75% of the investment's uptick. Instead of holding on for the other 25%, could you put your money somewhere else and get greater returns? If you do decide to stay in this investment, make sure to move your sell-stops (see Chapter 11) to lock in the profits you have already made. In the case of options, adjust your mental sell-stops upwards.

➢ **If the investment drops below your predetermined acceptable loss level,** as indicated by sell-stops or mental sell-stops. As I said in Chapter 11, I like to limit my losses to 10% of the price of a stock when I bought it, and 50% of the price of an option. So if I bought General Electric (GE) shares at $45, I'd put a sell-stop in at around $40. If I bought an option for $2, I'd sell it if it dropped to $1.

As I said earlier, in every market there are investments that will make you money, even if your current ones are not. Don't be afraid to take your licks and go where the money is.

# Defense Strategies: Covered Calls

In a covered call, you sell a call on a stock you currently own. If the price of the stock increases beyond the strike price of the call you sold, you will be exercised. If you want to keep the stock, you can simply buy the call back. You'll lose the profit from the call, but you'll get to keep your stock (which is now more valuable). You should wait until the very last day before the call expires to buy it back, because it will be cheapest then. I must say, however, I almost never choose to buy back a call I wrote on a covered call. The reason I wrote the call in the first place was to gain the income from the call, plus the potential capital gains from selling the stock. So why would I cancel out the transaction and lose money?

There are four principles I follow when writing covered calls, two of which you'll find listed in Chapter 24, "Ten Commandments of Investing." First, *don't fall in love with your investments. Learn to sell if necessary.* I only write covered calls on stock I'm perfectly willing to be called away on. There are some stocks on which I would never write covered calls because I'm not willing to sell them. Second, *Don't get greedy.* Buying back the option because the stock is running up (and because you probably believe it will run up further) is silly, in my opinion. Set your strike price at a price point where you'd be happy to sell the stock. Be satisfied with your profits on the call and the capital gains on your stock, and look for something else to invest in. Third, *choose stocks for this strategy following the guidelines described in Chapter 16.* You want some volatility in the stock price, but not a huge amount. The stock should be of good quality, and be trading at a price point of between $10 and $40 a share. Fourth and most important, *remember that covered call writing is a momentum, income-producing strategy.* These stocks should not form the core of your buy and hold portfolio. You must be willing to sell the stock and take your profits.

Now, what happens if the price of the stock suddenly drops below the level of your sell-stop (usually 10% less than you paid for the stock originally) before the call option expires? You want to get rid of the stock but you can't until the call on those shares expires. In this case, you buy the call back (at a lower price, as its value will have declined as the price of the stock went down), and then sell your stock immediately, hopefully at the level of your buy-stop order. You'll keep the premium from the original call (minus whatever you paid to buy it back) and you're out of the stock with a 10% loss instead of a larger one.

# Options Defense Strategies

I want to give you some very specific options trades defense strategies. Remember, our first principle is, do the opposite. If you bought a call or put, sell it. If you sold one, buy it back. But there are a few other things to note as well.

If you bought a call option and the price of the underlying stock drops, then the price of the option will drop, too. Sell the call immediately to recoup as much of your investment as possible. If you feel the price of the stock will continue to decline, consider buying a put so you can make money while the price decreases. However, if you believe in your original premise—that the price of the stock will go up before the option expires—you might actually consider buying additional calls, to lower your cost basis and increase your potential for profitability.

Here are other ways to defend yourself.

➢ **If you *bought* a call option and the stock price is falling, you can...**

1. *Sell the call* before it drops too far (absolutely sell it if it drops below 50% of what you paid for it)

2. *Buy more calls* if you believe the drop in price is temporary and it will rise before the calls expire (thus lowering your cost basis in this transaction)

3. *Buy a put* if you think the stock price will keep dropping. The money you make on the put will compensate for the loss on the call.

➢ **If you *bought* a put option and the stock price is rising, you can...**

1. *Sell the put* before its value drops too far (absolutely sell it if it drops below 50% of what you paid for it)

2. *Buy more puts* if you believe the rise in the stock price is temporary and it will drop

again before the puts expire (thus lowering your cost basis in this transaction)

3. *Buy a call* if you think the stock price will keep rising. The money you make on the call will compensate for the loss on the put.

4. *Sell a put* at a strike price lower than you believe the stock's price will drop. That way, you bring in a small amount of profit to offset any losses you may have.

➤ **If you** *sold* **a naked call option and the stock price is rising, you can** *buy the call back.* As the stock price rises, the call price will rise, too, so you might have to take a loss. Again, wait until the day the call expires so you are paying as little as possible. But remember, if your call is exercised, you'll have to buy stock at market value to cover the call. It might be smarter (and cheaper) simply to buy the call back.

➤ **If you** *sold* **a put option and the stock price is falling, you can** *buy the put back.* Again, try to buy it as cheaply as possible. Or if you're comfortable with purchasing the underlying stock at the put's strike price, you can let yourself be exercised. Remember, you made money by selling the put in the first place, so you've essentially bought the stock at a discount from the strike price anyway.

The simplest thing to remember with defensive strategies is, you can always get out of a position. Your goal is to get out with the smallest amount of loss and the greatest amount of profit possible, and hopefully to do so quickly. There are thousands of opportunities for your money to make money, no matter what's happening in the overall market. The key is to keep your head, manage your emotions, cut your losses, learn from your mistakes and your successes, and *move on.*

# 24

# Ten Commandments
# of Investing

### ~ 1 ~
**Diversify, diversify and then diversify!**

### ~ 2 ~
**Buy on weakness—sell on strength.**

### ~ 3 ~
**Maximize profits and limit losses
with stop orders.**

### ~ 4 ~
**Don't let your ego get in the way
of good decisions.**

~ 5 ~

**Don't fall in love with your investments.
Learn to sell if necessary.**

~ 6 ~

**Don't get greedy!**

~ 7 ~

**Think short-term: "How much can
I make this week?"**

~ 8 ~

**Do your homework.
Investigate and research.**

~ 9 ~

**If investment parameters change, get out!**

~ 10 ~

**Never, ever risk more than you can
afford to lose.**

# Appendix

# Glossary

| At the money | An option contract where the strike price is *equal* to the current price of the stock. |
|---|---|
| Call | An option contract giving the option holder the right but not the obligation to *buy* the underlying company stock at a specific price for a certain period of time. |
| Class | A group of options consisting of either puts or calls. |
| Contract | The minimum trading unit for options. Each contract represents 100 shares of stock in the underlying company. |
| Covered | An option term meaning that an option writer owns, or has the right to buy, the underlying stock of a particular company on which he has sold the right to purchase it to someone else (see *naked*). |

| | |
|---|---|
| **Discount** | The rate that the Federal Reserve Board charges member banks for borrowing funds. An increase in the rate is an attempt to restrict the money supply to ward off inflationary pressures. |
| **DJIA** | The Dow Jones Industrial Average, a weighted index representing the underlying prices (values) of common stock of 30 large U.S. companies. |
| **Dollar Cost Averaging** | Putting a certain amount of money each month, or at regular intervals, in a particular investment. You invest the same amount whether the investment is higher or lower priced at the time. Your cost per share, bond, etc. averages out over the length of your investment. |
| **Exercise** | The right of an option holder to require an option seller to deliver the underlying stock for purchase at the strike price. |
| **In the money** | A call option contract where the strike price is *below* the current price of the underlying stock, or a put option contract where the strike price is *above* the current price of the underlying stock. |

| | |
|---|---|
| **Margin** | Borrowing money from a brokerage firm or bank to purchase securities, which then act as collateral for the loan. |
| **Naked** | A term meaning that an option writer does not own or have the prior right to buy the underlying stock, although he has sold the right to purchase it to someone else (opposite of *covered*). |
| **Option** | A contract (representing 100 shares of stock) that gives the holder the right, but not the obligation, to buy or sell the underlying stock at a certain price (the strike price) for a specific period of time. |
| **Out of the money** | A call option where the strike price is *above* the current price of the stock, or a put option where the strike price is *below* the current price of the stock. |
| **Put** | An option which gives the holder the right, but not the obligation, to *sell* the underlying company stock at a specific price for a certain period of time. |

| **Spread** | The purchase of an option contract and sale of another option contract of the same class, at two different strike prices. Also, the difference between the bid price and the ask price in a stock quote. |
| --- | --- |
| **Straddle** | An option strategy involving the purchase of both a put and a call on the same stock with the same strike price and expiration. |
| **Strangle** | An option strategy involving the purchase of a put *below* the current price of the underlying stock and the purchase of a call *above* the current price, both having the same expiration date. |
| **Strike price** | The price at which the holder of an option contract can exercise his right to buy or sell the underlying stock. |
| **Write** | An option term synonymous with the word *sell*. The sale can be either covered or naked depending upon the writer's ownership of the underlying stock. |
| **Zero Coupon Bond** | A derivative debt security that pays no interest and sells at a deep discount to maturity (face) value. |